CHANGE THE STORY OF YOUR HEALTH

~

USING SHAMANIC AND JUNGIAN TECHNIQUES FOR HEALING

CARL GREER, PhD, PsyD

FINDHORN PRESS

Published in 2017 by Findhorn Press, Scotland

ISBN 978-1-84409-716-6

Edited by Nicky Leach
Cover and interior design by Damian Keenan
Printed in the USA

Published by
Findhorn Press
117-121 High Street,
Forres IV36 1AB,
Scotland, UK

t +44 (0)1309 690582
f +44 (0)131 777 2711
e info@findhornpress.com
www.findhornpress.com

"Change the Story of Your Health is beautifully written and a gem for any reader who is looking to empower themselves, their health and their lives. We all have two general stories that we choose to live by: the story of our suffering and the story of our growth. You have the power to access your own story of growth and healing, should you choose. Dr. Carl Greer weaves for you the wisdom of the healing traditions to provide you with the tools to create a new story of health, one that is full of love, healing and insight. Read this book and change your story."

— EVA SELHUB, MD, author of *Your Health Destiny* and *Your Brain on Nature*
and Adjunct Scientist in the Neuroscience Laboratory at the Jean Mayer USDA
Human Nutrition Research Center on Aging at Tufts University

"As an academic physician who has been on a journey of self-discovery for most of my life, I am delighted to find a work as clear and understandable as Carl Greer's *Change the Story of Your Health*. Dr. Greer has created a remarkably accessible work offering fresh tools for self-exploration. The writing is frank and clear, and it feels as if he is speaking directly to the reader. Carl's voice resonates in each sentence, conveying his deep integrity and desire to be of service to others. The book covers a wide range of topics from shamanic journeying to the chakra system to the concept of the Quiet, a place where all possibilities and knowledge that have not yet taken form can be accessed. The reader is offered approaches to self-discovery intended to provide insights into the profound life lessons offered to each of us through our health stories.

This book is written for seekers who are searching for a fresh approach to self-understanding and looking for new ways to connect with Source for the purpose of healing. While several of the exercises are drawn from age-old or traditional methods of communicating with one's inner teachers and guides, Dr. Greer has his own take on them, so they will feel new and personal to many. But, the reader must remember that the printed word is just the starting place—intentional application and some practice are needed to gain insights into the self and what lies behind one's personal health story. The exercises can become part of one's spiritual practices without extensive instruction, and can be wisely used to delve deeper into the hidden currents flowing behind the scenes in each of our lives, currents that can have a profound effect on our behaviors and health.

Change the Story of Your Health is suitable for novice and experienced seekers alike. Reading it and using its techniques can serve as a first step in changing our relationship to our lives and our health."

— DAVID M. STEINHORN, MD, Professor of Pediatrics, Children's National Health System, Washington, DC, Medical Director, Pediatric Palliative Care and Attending Physician, Pediatric Intensive Care

Contents

Disclaimer

This book does not prescribe treatment for any specific psychological, medical, or physical condition. The information contained herein is provided as a public service. It is included for informational and educational purposes only and should not be construed as personal medical advice and should not be used for diagnosing or treating a medical or emotional problem or condition.

Always seek professional advice with any questions you may have regarding a particular medical or psychological issue. Reliance on any information provided in this book is solely at your own risk; the publisher and author assume no responsibility for your actions. Nothing in this book is designed to cure specific physical or psychological disorders or diseases.

The practices in this book can complement treatments you are receiving from medical and psychological health care providers. Check with your health care providers about the appropriateness of using these practices in tandem with the treatment you are receiving.

Stories of individuals' work with the ideas in this book have had details altered to protect confidentiality.

Acknowledgments

As I get older, like many of my peers, I'm spending more time dealing with health issues. With an ever-increasing number of health experts offering advice, and more specialists, procedures, medications, and treatments becoming available every day, making choices about health can feel overwhelming at times. But I know that each of us has a much greater ability than we think to learn from our symptoms, understand what our bodies need, and access our inner healer. Then our health story can be rewritten to be more satisfying.

Many of my writings and teachings over the years have been devoted to guiding people in accessing transpersonal realms to gain information and energy that can help them in their quest for personal transformation. I would like to acknowledge the shamans around the world I have worked with, in particular Alberto Villoldo, Theo Paredes, and Marv and Shanon Harwood. I would also like to acknowledge my doctor friends, including Sharon Martin, Shelley Stelzer, Melinda Ring, Wendy Dimmette, David Steinhorn, Rebecca Ratcliff, and Scott Kolbaba. They have supported me in my beliefs in the power of holistic medicine and the still unknown mysteries of healing. My Jungian friends who have influenced me over the years include the late Lee Roloff as well as Murray Stein, Mary Dougherty, and James Wyly. All of them have been allies in my developing a greater understanding of and respect for the energy of the transpersonal realms and its potential for helping us to heal.

I would also like to thank those who helped in the preparation of this book. Nancy Peske's insights and editorial guidance were invaluable. Charlotte Kelchner and Heather Booton assisted me in organizing a large amount of seemingly disjointed material. Gladys Burow, my administrative assistant for nearly 50 years, helped me prepare numerous drafts of this book.

I want to acknowledge my children, Caryn, Michael, and Janet, and my stepchildren, Michael, Susie, and Jeannie, as well as their significant others, Rudy, Jenny, Joe, Leslie, and Mike, who have all been part of my journey.

I also want to acknowledge Pat—my love, my wife, and my partner in exploring the symbolic and literal realms of our lives. She has supported my esoteric explorations and my devoting time to writing *Change the Story of Your Health*. Her careful reading of the drafts and her comments helped make this book better.

Finally, I am grateful that Spirit has given me the opportunity to live a story that has lasted many years and brought me great satisfaction and allowed me to share some of what I have learned with others.

Dedication

To all who yearn to discover their inner healer
and connect with larger energies that can help them
in their quest for wellness.

Foreword

In our time on this planet, we come across people who have a profound influence on our lives. Through these meetings the path we are on can be diverted, make a U-turn or go places we don't anticipate. Dr. Carl Greer has been for me one of those pivotal people.

I first met Carl through my role at Northwestern Medicine as director of the Osher Center for Integrative Medicine. Our program, started in 1997, was one of the first centers within an academic health center to offer integrative care, combining conventional Western medicine with other healing disciplines under one roof. When I became director in 2007, I had a vision of developing the Center into something that could help shift the current disease-care system into one that valued and promoted true health in all its facets. I was introduced to Carl as someone with a similar ethos who wanted to help us achieve our goals. Carl brought a unique potpourri of spiritual connection through his shamanic work, philanthropic support, intuitive understanding of human nature honed as a result of his training in Jungian psychology, and practical business sense developed over the course of his successful career. We have worked together to implement medical education offerings such as an elective to teach medical students mind-body skills so they can cope with the stresses of training to become a physician, and a grand rounds series bringing the latest findings in integrative medicine research to our academic health system. Carl has also been instrumental in the creation of several charitable programs to promote access to integrative disciplines such as acupuncture, naturopathic medicine and yoga within underserved populations who might otherwise not be able to afford it.

As I got to know Carl, I came to respect him immensely for his vision, thoughtfulness, generosity and intelligence. I also began to learn about his own evolution and the studying he had done in America and abroad with sacred healers and shamans. Carl shared the work he was doing to bring his shamanic trainings to helping health professionals approach their work from a different perspective. He invited me to several retreats, but I deferred for a couple of years, claiming too many commitments to work and family. But really I was a bit skeptical because it seemed so far from my academic roots, and was too "unknown." As time passed, Carl become both a mentor and friend. I reached a place in my personal growth where I had come across a block and needed to decide whether to try to break through it or just keep rolling along in the same way. I decided to accept Carl's invitation to a shamanic retreat and traveled to a lodge along with nineteen other people for a four-day immersion in shamanism and personal work.

During the retreat, Carl led us on "journeys" to explore the stories of our past, current and future selves. The first two days of our group work were interesting, though not earth-shattering for me. Then, on the third day, Carl introduced an exercise to take us outside our intellectual brain into emotion with the simple task of writing down the name of a song that represented our past life and our future life. As someone who was never a music addict or good with names, I halfheartedly jotted down the titles of two songs that had stuck with me, that for whatever reason connected with something in me: The past story song I chose was "Fireflies" by Owl City; the future story song was "Solsbury Hill" by Peter Gabriel. Later that afternoon, I went for a solitary walk in the woods before dinner and decided to listen to "Fireflies" to see if there could possibly be any message for me. As I listened on repeat fifteen or so times without any insights, I decided (the wonder of modern technology) to Google the meaning of song. As I read through interpretations of this seemingly joyful, playful song and how it was a message about the loss of childhood innocence, something broke in me. Sobbing, with arms out to my sides, open to the woods around me, I cried for an hour—something I hadn't done for decades. Finally, drained, I sat under a tree in the fall leaves and put on the song of my future story: "Solsbury Hill." A quick search revealed that Peter Gabriel has said of the song's meaning, "It's about being prepared to lose what you have for what you might get, or what you are for what you might be. It's about letting go." I finally understood what Carl meant about being willing to get information from different places, messages that we are meant to hear even when we try to resist them.

As a result of this awakening, the past few years have been challenging in many ways. I've delved into some of the issues that have been holding me back over the years, including difficult events and emotions that I had sequestered rather than confront. But now as the arc of this transition comes to a close for me, the pieces of my past and present have become integrated within me, opening space for exciting things in the future.

I know I am only one of so many people who have benefitted from Carl's wisdom and his ability to hold people in a safe space without judgment or persuasion. In this book, Carl's voice resonates in every written word. Readers who are willing to open their hearts and minds to the potential for new learning can transform stories about themselves that no longer serve them into new stories of wholeness and possibility. This text deals with the important topic of the stories we carry about our own health. We may develop these stories out of a sense that we are born with a genetic destiny and our health history is preordained. Other stories are written through experiences with our health that bring us face-to-face with our mortality at vulnerable times in our life. And other stories that we have held precious must change when we receive a new diagnosis and we are challenged to envision a future that is different than expected, yet still beautiful. Throughout this book, Carl weaves in true stories from his patients, journal prompts, and instructions for shamanic journeys, providing a practical guide to understanding your relationship to your health story.

Many people suffer when they define themselves by their illnesses and by traumatic experiences related to their concepts of health and mortality. Healing isn't just something that comes from medicine or surgeries; it comes from a shift in the way we perceive ourselves and our connection to our health and our bodies. The mind is powerful; our thoughts and beliefs make a difference in how we feel and how we respond to threats to our well-being. It is possible to create new stories or views of ourselves that not only change our emotional well-being but also our physical health. I am honored to be a small part of bringing Carl's influence to others. I hope that through this enlightening book, many can experience the deep and transformative blessings he has given to me and my family.

MELINDA RING, MD, FACP
Executive Director, Northwestern Medicine Osher Center for Integrative Medicine
Clinical Associate Professor of Medicine and Medical Social Sciences,
Northwestern University Feinberg School of Medicine
Coauthor of *The Natural Menopause Solution* and
Coeditor of *Integrative Medicine, An Issue of Primary Care*

Preface

What is healing? What is health? Perhaps we each would define these terms differently. Most of us tend to take health for granted until we become injured or develop an illness or a disease that we have to manage. Then, we are likely to define "healing" as a return to our previous state of wellness. However, a return to the past may feel impossible.

"Healing" may mean adjusting to a new health story that you seem to be living. On the other hand, it may mean a recommitment to wellness that results in you becoming healthier than you have ever been.

What if, despite aging, injuries, health conditions, and illnesses, you could not only return to the state of health you enjoyed previously but even improve on it? If your goal is to live well for many decades to come, you might want to see any health challenges you have as offering opportunities for attaining greater vitality, strength, and stamina. Maybe you can develop deeper appreciation for your body and the pleasure it gives you and have a better relationship with it—and a better relationship with any conditions you have. Whatever losses you might experience as a result of of menopause, andropause, and aging, being on a healing path could render them far less devastating than they would be otherwise. A focus on health and healing—emotionally, mentally, and spiritually, as well as physically—can bring gifts you might never have known you were missing.

While this book is about health, it is also about healing in whatever way you define it. The techniques you will learn will affect you at many levels. As a Jungian analyst and shamanic practitioner, I have been privileged to spend thousands of hours engaged in healing work with others, individually and in groups. I have learned to appreciate the ability that each of us has for self-healing. Countless times I have witnessed the power of the stories people tell about themselves, the events of their lives, and their struggles and triumphs. In my private practice, as well as in workshops I have led, I have seen the kinds of transformations that take place when people actively take control of their stories and work with techniques for transformation that are drawn from shamanic traditions and Jungianism.

In my previous book, *Change Your Story, Change Your Life: Using Shamanic and Jungian Tools to Achieve Personal Transformation*, I offered practices that could help people explore their life's story, choose a more desirable one, and bring that new story into being. Within any life story is a story of health, and I have come to realize that many who read my previous book were concerned with health and healing from a holistic, mind-body-spirit perspective.

In this book, some of the practices are new and some are similar to the ones in my earlier book. However, this time, the spotlight is on writing and bringing to life a new health story, and specifically, on:

- improving health and well-being
- maintaining wellness as you age
- managing chronic conditions
- dealing with having your health story suddenly rewritten by events you did not expect (such as accidents and diagnoses of conditions or diseases).

Many aspects of your personal story—including your relationships, your emotions and moods, your job or vocation, and your connection to God, Spirit, Source, or a higher power—can affect the story of your health, which can, in turn, affect these other areas of your life. We all know that being ill, feeling run down, or having to manage the symptoms of a disease can make it very hard to be giving and attentive in our relationships, feel positive and optimistic, and find the energy and focus to address challenges at work. Conversely, health improvements can lead to a better larger story. Having more endurance, fewer acute ailments, and less physical discomfort or pain can make it easier to remain active, experience greater well-being, and focus on other aspects of your life that require your attention.

Throughout these pages, you will find practices that can help you improve your experience of your health. Even if you have a chronic health condition, these practices can help you to better live with it and experience a sense of wholeness and greater life satisfaction. The overall goals of the practices are to help you make and maintain healthy lifestyle changes through enhancing your connections to the invisible energetic realms that surround and infuse the material world. These connections allow you to access insights and energies that can bring to life a new story of your health.

There is another payoff to changing the story of your health that you might not have considered: it can help you to contribute to the wholeness and health of society by affecting the energy field we all share. You might see these effects in people in your life who become inspired to ask you about the practices you are using and start working with them on their own. Once you develop a greater sense of health and well-being, you might see differences in how others interact with you. However, changes you bring about in the larger, shared energy field may be invisible to you. Perhaps you will sense them when you are in an altered state of consciousness brought about by one of the expanded-awareness practices, such as shamanic journeying, that you will find in this book.

Whenever I do healing work, I feel blessed to be part of a mystery that is bigger than myself or my clients. I often am touched by the insights, experiences, and blessings they have and share with me. I believe there are forces in us and around us that are available to help us heal if we invite them in and are open to them. The healing we do becomes a part of our health stories.

My Own Story

My story of becoming a psychologist, Jungian analyst, and shamanic practitioner has been circuitous. On my father's maternal side, going back generations, there were many doctors on the family tree, and I could have chosen to walk that path. I had interests in the liberal arts, psychology, and spirituality, but felt I should study metallurgical engineering and become a businessman like my father, who worked in the steel industry. That choice seemed practical and safe—and as so many do, I repressed my sense of adventure and daring.

I eventually earned a doctorate in finance and management, and taught at Columbia University's Graduate School of Business before moving to Chicago and going to work for an independent oil company. I was happy and successful, but the urge to become a healer stirred in me again. This time, I paid attention and chose to change the focus of my career. I remained involved in the business world but earned a doctorate in clinical psychology and became a licensed clinical psychologist, a Jungian analyst, and later, a shamanic practitioner.

For me, the call to help others heal did not come as a result of illness or an accident that made me question what I was doing or where I was going. However, you might find that health challenges are pushing you to explore new ways of relating to any physical challenges you have. These explorations may lead you to heal in ways you had never considered: healing your aching heart. Healing your fear of stepping outside of a story scripted by your parents or your community. Healing your unhealthy relationship with your body. Healing your longing for a relationship with a higher power, so that you feel you have the security of something larger than yourself looking out for you. The list of possibilities is long.

Being a healer gives me a strong sense of purpose and a relationship with a higher power. For that, I am grateful. I may have been a late bloomer in some ways, but I believe people are called to a spiritual life and to their soul's purpose when they are ready. The "whys" and "whens" may not seem clear at the time and only partially understood in retrospect.

My understanding of my purpose deepened one day, more than sixteen years ago, while walking on a beach. I experienced a spontaneous sense of being connected with each of the natural elements—water, fire, earth, and air—more deeply than I ever had been. I became aware that they were not inert but rather had a consciousness I could engage. That experience, combined with having just read the book *Shaman, Healer, Sage* by Alberto Villoldo, PhD, led me to pursue shamanic training at his Healing the Light Body School and later, to join their staff as a teacher.

My shamanic practices helped me revise my story in many ways and drove my desire to go deeper into shamanic studies. I have since studied and worked with shamans in South America, the United States, Canada, Australia, Ethiopia, and Outer Mongolia, and shared experiences and exchanged worldviews with them. We agreed that we all come from and return to Source (the creative force of the universe) and that we and everything else is infused by Source. We also agreed that when we do healing work, it is really Source and our clients who do the work—our role is to create conditions for healing to occur. What that healing entails is not for me to decide; my role is simply to help others to heal in whichever ways they define "healing."

I now spend my time writing, teaching, engaging in philanthropic and business activities, and working with clients as a clinical psychologist, Jungian analyst, and shamanic practitioner. I live in Chicago with my wife, Pat. I have three children, three stepchildren, and fourteen grandchildren. My story was not one I would have predicted when I was determined to push aside my interests in psychology and liberal arts, but by honoring the hidden forces and wisdom within me that knew where I could go with my life, I ended up where I needed to be.

Now that I am in the later years of my life, the story of my health is drawing my attention more than it did decades ago. I work with the practices in this book to ensure that my health story continues to be one that is satisfying to me. My hope is that these practices, and the approach to healing I offer in this book, lead you to greater health and well-being, and to healing, however you define it.

Introduction

Throughout the world, the idea of a universal, interconnected grid composed of energy, where we can access insights and energies that affect the physical body as well as the psyche, is a part of many healing traditions. Many of them recognize a physical world and an unseen world of consciousness and energy that seem to be separated but, in fact, are always intertwined. It is easier to perceive the interconnections between these realms when we are not bogged down by the limitations of ordinary awareness.

Why does it matter what is beyond what the conscious mind can observe? The existence of an unseen world and what lies within it may be important not only to our physical health but for healing mentally, emotionally, and spiritually. The promise of energy medicine and practices that involve expanded awareness—practices that can be found in Jungianism, shamanism, and other traditions and which you will discover in this book—is that we can access and work with these hidden insights and energies to heal what ails us.

We do not know, perceive, or understand all the relationships among the visible world, the invisible world, and the energy matrixes that scientists recognize, including the electromagnetic field. I believe that while some of these matrixes and connections may be too subtle for our current technologies to identify, they are nevertheless real. These energy environments may be the invisible realms that philosophers, shamans, and spiritual believers recognize. We may someday discover that what science acknowledges and what healers and philosophers understand have more in common than we might think. We may come to better appreciate the incredible power of expanded-awareness practices for working with these fields to improve our health.

To engage invisible realms, we can incorporate techniques from Jungianism as well as from shamanism as practiced by healers in various cultures. All across the globe, there are shamans who recognize a unified energy field and work with the energies of nature and with transpersonal realms—places we can all experience that exist in another reality and are accessible only by shifting one's consciousness into a trancelike state.

Shamans make this shift while maintaining their own will and personal consciousness. While in those states, they travel to and interact with transpersonal realms in order to gain information and energy for healing work they do for themselves and others. Then, they bring the information and energy back into ordinary reality in the present. The essence of shamanic healing is to work with our past so that it lives within us differently and we no longer are caught in old habits—and to align with a future that is more desirable for us and Spirit. By working with the past and future in this way, we make better decisions in the present.

You can learn to be your own shaman through discipline, focus, and practice, as well as a willingness to recognize the value of shamanism beyond merely fixing problems in the physical realm. Shamanic work awakens a person to greater awareness of the interconnectedness of all that is seen and unseen. That, in turn, often leads to a greater sense of healing than merely addressing health issues using allopathic (Western) medicine. Healing, from the same root word as "whole," may involve reintegrating into your life what was lost or forgotten and what your soul cries out for, whether it is a renewed sense of worthiness, mystery, joy, or purpose.

We all have heard of the mind-body connection, but how strong is it? Shamans believe that energetic and spiritual imbalances are at the root of all physical ailments. Consequently, shamanic tradition involves identifying and then fixing or healing these imbalances or blockages in a person's energy system. Several of the practices you will find here—such as cleansing your chakras—involve manipulating energy for the purpose of healing. Qigong, acupuncture, and other traditions for healing and wellness, like shamanism and chakra healing, fall under the umbrella category of energy medicine. For me, energy medicine fits well with the tradition of Jungian psychology. Jungians work with clients to identify, address, and heal the underlying psychological issues that can affect behaviors, attitudes, beliefs, and emotions. Ultimately, because of the mind-body connection, Jungian psychological techniques may contribute to improved physical health.

Undoubtedly, the scientific and medical worlds have developed a wealth of valuable health information and tools for treatment. However, we are starting to return our attention to what might have been lost as Western medicine became more concerned with surgeries and pharmaceutical medicines than more traditional healing approaches.

In my opinion, using energy medicine in conjunction with modalities such as Western medicine, Chinese medicine, Ayurvedic medicine, acupuncture, psychotherapy, and chiropractic work can lead to better health and wellness. These approaches complement lifestyle interventions, such as managing stress and changing eating and exercise habits.

Although the effectiveness of energy healing can't be proven by double-blind research studies, there is evidence to support it, which you can read about in this book's afterword. When energy medicine appears to work, the good results could be due to a variety of variables. The altered state or trance you experience when using a shamanic technique could in some way contribute to healing, regardless of any specific practice used by a shamanic practitioner—or you—during a healing session. Also, your condition may have been arrested or started to reverse itself due to some unidentified factor rather than from the energy medicine. The placebo effect could contribute to the positive outcome. However, if the interventions are noninvasive, cost nothing (of course, they would be free if you used them on yourself), and can be employed to address a number of ailments for which we don't have simple solutions in the form of a pill or an operation, I see no downside to using expanded-awareness practices and energy medicine. In fact, given that they can also lead to a greater sense of well-being and a deeper connection to Source, I dedicate time to helping others learn about these healing modalities.

The exercises I recommend in this book are all ones you can do on your own as a complement to any other healing practices you are using. When a condition is serious, I don't recommend using shamanic and Jungian techniques, or any of the expanded-awareness practices I offer, to replace Western medicine. Instead, I suggest using a combination of allopathic and complementary techniques and being honest with your physician or physicians about what you are doing and experiencing.

I follow my own advice. Some years ago, I had a stent placed in a blocked artery in my left kidney. Two years later, a test showed that an artery in my right kidney was blocked. This time, rather than scheduling an operation right away, I worked on the blockage energetically with the intention to clear it so I would not need surgery. The next kidney scan showed no sign of blockage.

I continued to work with my doctor to monitor the health of my kidneys and my overall health and let him know what was working for me. I was forthright with him about my use of energy medicine.

If you are dealing with an occasional, acute ailment, such as a pain of known origin, you might want to use the practices in this book as your primary intervention before seeing a physician. I suggest you work closely with a medical practitioner who respects the use of expanded-awareness practices for healing. Doing so will help you gauge when you need to consult your physician and when you can simply begin addressing a particular physical problem by using these techniques.

You are the one who must decide how to use the material in this book most effectively to enhance your health and well-being. See yourself as the single subject in your own research study. You have a unique health situation, unique genetics, and unique experiences and proclivities. You must customize everything, and check in with yourself to determine whether the practices are helpful for you in writing a new story of your health.

You get to decide how often you work with the practices you find here, and whether to use them regularly or only occasionally. You are the one who will determine which healers, including doctors, you will partner with in your quest to awaken your own body's capacity for self-healing and thus experience better health and wellness. A healer others highly admire and recommend may not be the right partner for you. Healers, such as doctors (from the Latin "docere" meaning "to teach"), therapists, acupuncturists, or nutritionists, can only teach you how to turn on your own body's capacity for self-healing. You must take responsibility for following through on your commitments to use techniques you believe can be helpful for self-healing. And you must be honest with yourself about your health story as it truly is right now, so that you can write a new one and begin to bring it into being.

Within each of us is a wise inner healer who is connected to the wisdom and power of Source and who can guide us in discovering what we need to do differently to improve our health and wellness. This inner healer represents our body's capacity for self-healing. As Andrew Weil, MD, wrote in his book *Spontaneous Healing*: "Even when treatments are applied with successful outcomes, those outcomes represent activation of intrinsic healing mechanisms which, under other circumstances, might operate without any outside stimulus.... The body can heal itself."[1]

Keep in mind that this book is not meant to be a replacement for medical treatment or advice. It is meant to guide you in accessing greater information that you may find helpful for transforming the story of your health. Never look solely to a shaman, analyst, counselor, or doctor to tell you what to do. If you are a healer treating others—a physician, clinical psychologist, Jungian analyst, shaman, energy medicine practitioner, and so forth—consider trying out these practices yourself. Your insights into how the practices have worked for you can assist you in better meeting the needs of those who come to you for healing. The last chapter in this book will help you discover more about working as a healer within a community while tending to your own health and wellness.

A Word about the Core Practices in This Book

In this book, you will learn how to do shamanic journeying and dialoguing, two important expanded-awareness practices. Dialoguing, a practice based in the Jungian technique of active imagination, can be done within a shamanic journey to a transpersonal realm, but it typically is done afterward, for the purpose of gaining insights and advantageous energies. In dialoguing, you pose questions, and your unconscious answers.

Dialoguing can be used with symbols, inner figures, emotions, health symptoms, your inner healer, the earth, the sky, your resistance to changing a habit that is affecting your health, and so on. You can also dialogue with what you encountered when dreaming or when using any number of expanded-awareness practices you find in this book, asking questions and receiving answers from your unconscious that provide insights. I invite you to be creative as you approach the expanded-awareness practices, keeping in mind their potential for helping you discard what no longer serves you and bring in what can help you in your quest for healing.

I encourage you to try all the practices in this book and use some or all of them regularly if you would like to make changes to your health story more quickly. Using the everyday-awareness practice of journaling will help you understand and remember what you learned and experienced when using the expanded-awareness practices. I suggest that you work with both types of practices for transforming your health story into one that is more satisfying.

All my experiences, personal and professional, have convinced me that it is truly possible to change the story of your health regardless of the challenges you face. I hope you will give it a try and see how the techniques in this book work for you.

CHAPTER ONE

Your Health Has a Story, and You Are the Storyteller

The physician came to my office in a southwestern suburb of Chicago after hearing through friends that I might be able to help her. Barbara had been diagnosed with cancer and was using all her resources in the medical field to attain the best possible care for her condition. Although trained in Western medicine and much invested in the powers of science, medicine, and the rational mind to bring about healing, Barbara wanted to explore a modality that might optimize her chances for a full recovery. She was a type-A, meticulous woman, who was attentive to every detail of her lab reports and medication orders; nevertheless, she was open to a completely different way of addressing her illness: through the non-rational mind.

Over the course of several two-hour sessions, I used shamanic and Jungian techniques to help Barbara shift out of ordinary consciousness and into expanded awareness. I knew this would help her to feel a sense of peace and to access the wisdom of her unconscious mind. According to psychologist Carl Jung, one of the founders of modern psychology, we can use these methods to tap into our personal unconscious, as well as the collective unconscious, where information and what he called archetypes reside. Engaging the unconscious allows us to gain insights about ourselves and our situations. It also lets us work with forces that affect what we experience and how we perceive and interpret those experiences.

The stories we tell ourselves and others are fashioned from events but also our perceptions and interpretations of them; one person's story of being diagnosed with cancer, treating it, and beating it might be very different from another person's story. Through shamanic and Jungian work, we can write new health stories for ourselves, reinterpreting the past and present and committing to a new future. We can overcome emotional obstacles to healing, such as shame and fear. My goal was to assist Barbara in writing and bringing to life a new story for her health. I also hoped I could help her see how her health story was interwoven with the story of her life and all its chapters.

Before she became ill, Barbara's health was excellent, and she had taken it for granted. She had not consciously chosen to write a story of her health that involved a cancerous tumor, but wondered if her type-A personality and constant drive to achieve had somehow contributed to her health crisis. By becoming conscious of her story, she empowered herself to change it. She told me she wanted to write and live according to a new story, one that would allow her to return to her previous state of physical well-being. I knew that if she and I worked with her non-rational mind, she might be able to trust at the deepest level that she was capable of living a healthy, long life, free of cancer and any belief systems that were not working for her. This could lead to an improved state of health.

In our sessions, we explored Barbara's worries about what might happen if the tumor continued to grow. What fate would befall her teenage children, who depended on her? Would she have the physical strength and the emotional and mental stamina to continue battling the cancer if her condition worsened? Would she have the courage to face the possibility of death, and if so, could she access this courage now?

I guided Barbara through visualizations and shamanic journeys that allowed her to face her fears in a way that she couldn't when she was in ordinary consciousness. These practices also allowed her to access her inner healer and its wisdom and energies, activating her ability to heal herself. She hoped her inner healer would begin to destroy the cancerous tumor. In the weeks that followed, as she waited for surgery to remove it, testing showed that the tumor had shrunk inexplicably. The surgeon removed what was left.

Barbara felt that becoming what she called a "master of her thoughts" and using visualization were what improved her condition and eventually allowed her to beat the cancer. It's possible that there was another reason the tumor shrank, but Barbara felt certain that the shamanic and Jungian work she did had played an important role in bringing to life a new, more positive story of her health.

The Power of Story

When it comes to our health, we all have a story to tell, just as we have stories about our relationships, psychology, and other aspects of our lives. Our health stories can involve acute illnesses and chronic conditions or diseases and feelings about how weak or strong, attractive or unattractive, or in shape or out of shape we are. Events and experiences—from aching joints to stiff neck muscles to lessened mobility due to arthritis or past injuries—can all weave into a health story. However, you might choose to write a new health story that includes improved energy and vitality, feeling more confident in your body's appearance, and greater stamina.

Your individual health story might have been very much influenced by cultural and family stories. Participants in support groups for people with health conditions are often surprised by how much overlap there is between their individual stories and those of others. Hearing about how someone else overcame their frustration with reduced mobility and stamina, or how they conquered their sense of their body betraying them, can serve as inspiration for someone who has not yet considered these perspectives or incorporated them into her own health story.

At the same time, cultural messages about aging, youth, beauty, and exercising can cause you to become out of touch with your own values and beliefs about your health. Your health story might be unduly influenced by peers who are not admitting that they, too, are afraid of aging, balding, losing vitality and attractiveness, and managing pain from joint deterioration that makes certain types of exercise difficult.

If you are like most of us, you are not always honest with yourself about the challenges you face regarding your health. You might say you feel good about your health story but actually be scared that you are not going to return to your previous state of health, that you are not going to lose the weight you gained or get back the vitality and stamina you had before you developed an autoimmune disorder.

You might tell yourself that going through menopause or andropause (the male hormonal shift at midlife) is not causing you any significant problems, when deep down you are embarrassed, confused, and upset that your sexual desire has been reduced, you feel less sexually attractive, and you are wrestling with fears about growing older and being seen as "washed up." Even people in their twenties can worry about aging, mortality, and being past their physical prime—particularly if they have had to deal with athletic injuries, cancer, or an accident that temporarily robbed them of their mobility and stamina.

Whatever your state of health, you do not have to live with your current, dissatisfying health story. By exploring it and any unconscious beliefs or feelings associated with it, you can work with your health story to improve it. You can alter your perceptions about your body and your health condition (if you have one). Doing so may lead to improved physical health as you start to understand your experiences and to change how your memories and perceptions affect your story—and your reality.

Why a Health "Story"?

As a Jungian analyst and shamanic practitioner, I use the language of "story" to describe what I am helping others to transform. I find the concept effective for framing a discussion of how we make sense of our past and present experiences and shape our future experiences. Stories incorporate themes that can help us to better comprehend what seems to simply happen to us, as well as why we act as we do. A cancer "sufferer" and a cancer "warrior" are two very different ways to describe what a person with a diagnosis of cancer is experiencing as she works to regain her health.

From our earliest days as humans, we shared stories around the fire to help create and maintain community bonds. As people tried to make sense of their experiences, they internalized commonly shared stories. Stories changed as different people retold them or interpreted them in new ways. Constant in those stories were themes anyone, even a modern person, could recognize. Jungians would call these archetypal themes—and would say they are embedded in archetypal stories (for example, stories of overcoming suffering or of forgetting the past and thus being doomed to repeat it).

My interest in stories goes back to my childhood, but as a boy, I did not fully appreciate the power in the folktales, myths, and legends I enjoyed. I loved stories of magic and heroes who saved vulnerable children and good people caught in circumstances beyond their control. The great folk stories and legends with themes of heroism, companionship, collaboration, and courage appealed to me. Many years later, as an adult, I returned again to the pleasure I experienced reading these tales. I started to recognize that the narratives we create to explain the events in our lives often contain common themes and events and plotlines present in these classic stories.

More than once in my life, I chose to change my personal story. I began to study Jungianism and later, shamanism. I learned new stories from cultures I had been unfamiliar with, and realized that stories and themes had energetic qualities that affect people's experiences. While Carl Jung wrote about archetypes that influence our lives, shamans spoke of energies that influence a person's health, beliefs, and emotions. I could see a connection between shamanism and Jungianism, a flowing together of wisdom that would influence my own story. I recognized that stories have power for healing and transformation.

Aspire to a Better Story of Your Health

No matter what your health story, no matter what challenging health conditions you may have, you can choose to be optimistic. Every day, there are breakthroughs in medical research and news about discoveries of effective treatments. We are learning more about disease processes and how to support immunity and increase the likelihood of healthy aging. We are coming to understand that digestion works differently as we age, for example, and that digestive issues can affect brain chemistry and mood.

This new information might yield options you had not considered, such as taking nutritional supplements to improve digestion and reduce depressive moods. We know that medications have side effects, and that while they can reduce symptoms of a chronic health condition, they often do not address its underlying causes, which can then lead to other symptoms. Medications also can conflict with each other, and deplete you of necessary nutrients, creating imbalances in the body and brain. By reconsidering the medications you take and eliminating some you no longer need, you might find yourself in better health.

The more you learn about health breakthroughs and look more closely at your health story, the more likely it is that you will find solutions to your health challenges. While you may not be able to reverse aging to the degree you might like, and certain physical ailments may turn out to be irreversible as well, you can make improvements—even very significant ones.

You can come to perceive your age and condition differently, and this change in attitude can contribute to better physical health, thanks to the mind–body connection. You may be able to write a new health story in which your condition is less of a problem for you, and perhaps even an asset in some ways.

Let's say you have fibromyalgia (a disease involving chronic muscular pain), which is exacerbated whenever you eat refined sugar—a food that also has long-term, negative effects on your entire body, causing weight gain and cellular inflammation. You might view those symptoms as helpful warnings to get back on track with eating well and taking care of yourself. Then, perhaps you will be inspired to write a story in which these symptoms play a positive role in your maintaining and even improving the state of your health. What would be your new health story if you still had the condition but weren't "suffering from" or "plagued by" it, and instead were managing it well?

Your body will inevitably change over time, but you do not have to participate in a story written by someone else—a story about how people with a particular condition or disease have myriad limitations, about how being overweight means not being healthy and active, or about experiencing a slow physical and mental decline simply because you are growing older. Also, much as you try to maintain good health, accidents happen, and it can be difficult to come back from injuries. Knowing techniques for achieving healing insights and energies can be of great value to you should you face these challenges.

It is natural to be concerned about only one particular health problem that bothers you, but remember that improvements in one area lead to improvements in another. A seemingly intractable problem may be solvable if you broaden your perspective and look at other aspects of your health and your life.

For example, many people are discovering that their mood, stamina, strength, and immunity improve when they remove processed sugar from their diets or repair a fractured relationship that is causing them mental and emotional stress. They may find that learning more about their health, and sharing what they have learned with others, helps them to feel a stronger sense of community, purpose, and service. All of that, in turn, may improve their mood and outlook, as well as reduce stress that can lead to sickness and disease. Taking a multifaceted approach to health may produce more far-reaching results than simply cutting sugar out of their diet.

There is more good news. It is easier than ever before to discover valuable information about health that you can use to help you make changes in your habits. The challenge is not just to set goals for better health and better habits but to discover and overcome any hidden obstacles to achieving them.

What Blocks You from Experiencing
a Satisfying Health Story?

Although you can control the way you choose to think about your health, you may experience some very real blocks to writing, bringing to life, and maintaining a satisfying health story. If you do not understand how your health problems are related to each other, and to the other aspects of your overall life story, you might not realize how important it is to change certain habits; you might not even be aware you have them.

Also, if you have a health condition and find it necessary to be treated by different specialists, those healers might not be communicating with each other, which can be frustrating and get in the way of achieving a better state of wellness. You and your team of healers can miss the overall big picture of your health, become bogged down in details, and overlook the larger themes and the connections between, say, eating a certain type of food and experiencing symptom flare-ups. Working with the story of your health can prevent a fragmented approach to health that can reduce the effectiveness of the various modalities and treatments you are using.

Ideally, you would have one person on your medical team who knows all of your issues and can coordinate on your behalf, as general physicians used to do. Unfortunately, too often these days, that isn't possible. You may need to assume more responsibility for your medical care than you feel qualified to do. I encourage you to work with healers collaboratively, making sure they know the facts about your situation and are aware of the choices you are making. Your team members may have different opinions about what you should do to improve your health, which can make you feel confused and frustrated. At the end of the day, checking in with your unconscious mind and working with its wisdom may help you to feel more confident in your choices and your ability to make the right decisions for you.

As daunting and stressful as it may be to take charge of the story of your health, and to have to deal with conflicting health information, keep in mind that there are benefits to taking in alternate viewpoints and ideas about health. When you use expanded-awareness practices and journaling to access your deep feelings and beliefs, you may find it easier to reconcile these different opinions.

As you look at your health story, do you find it satisfying? Have you come to overidentify with it, and given up on the potential for changing it? Are you afraid of your health story rewriting itself in ways that make you unhappy? For example, do you fear changes that will come with aging?

What if you had a new health story with which to identify, one in which you were a rejuvenated, powerful, and re-energized conqueror of your medical condition?

Identifying with Your Health Story

Most of us identify with our thought processes and emotional experiences. We might say about ourselves, "I am a shy introvert" or "I'm a people person." However, we might not realize how much we identify with our physical selves and our current state of health. Typically, we don't identify with illnesses unless we develop a pattern of distress and write a story in which we are a "chronic migraine sufferer" or "a person with a weak constitution" or "someone who has always had a weak stomach." The language we use to describe our experiences is worth considering.

The names of diagnoses have power, too. For example, waking up during the night and having trouble falling back to sleep can seem more serious and hard to address if you think of it as "insomnia" and yourself as "someone who is battling insomnia." You might choose to observe the change in your sleep pattern and learn more about it, so that you can work around it and begin to think about it differently. Perhaps you will decide to journal or read if you can't get back to sleep after a few minutes, using the time productively. You might look more closely at how much sleep you need and find solutions that you wouldn't have thought of if you were simply focused on "overcoming insomnia" and sleeping straight through the night consistently. Letting go of the term "insomnia" might reduce your worry that having this "condition" means your sleep will be inadequate and you will always be groggy during the day.

As we start to develop chronic ailments and experience reduced flexibility and balance, decreased strength and physical stamina, and the symptoms of aging and disease, we may start to identify with the illnesses we are experiencing and lose faith that we can cure or overcome them. I have noticed this in my work and try to help people find new identities and write new stories for themselves after they have become convinced that their health condition is unchangeable, even though that isn't necessarily the case.

If you feel you can't change your story, it can seem comforting to identify with it. Seeing yourself as "a diabetic" or "an asthma sufferer" could offer certain payoffs depending on the health story you write. Those payoffs might include receiving sympathy from others, getting out of social situations you would rather avoid, or being part of a group of people who share a common experience of having diabetes. The payoffs might also include excuses for why you haven't been productive and achieved the goals you set for yourself. You might not even be conscious of these payoffs; if you were, you might decide there are better ways to achieve your goals and feel a sense of control over your life. Expanded-awareness practices can bring to light unconscious obstacles to achieving better health.

The truth is you are not your condition, your disease, or your pain, and you might have more power to manage them than it appears on the surface. You can relate to any condition differently. When you identify with your health challenges, you lose your ability to work with them, and they begin to control you and dictate what your health story is.

Sickness or disease can make you doubt whether you will ever be able to return to your previous state of wellness or even improve upon it. Uncertainty about your physical health and mortality can make you even more aware of your mortality and question whether you have enough time left to do all you would like to do. Although these topics can be painful to explore, they can also lead to transformation. So, for example, men who are dealing with prostate cancer and women who are dealing with the loss of a breast due to cancer may feel they have lost their sexuality and sexual attractiveness. Realizing that sexuality encompasses more than what they once thought can free them of the old story of their health that isn't working for them and perhaps give them more confidence in themselves and their attractiveness. They can fashion a new, more empowering identity around their new beliefs and their new experiences.

As you work on changing the story of your health, you might find it difficult to imagine a health story that does not include physical ailments or symptoms of a chronic health condition. Maybe what you desire is impossible, so your new health story will include a theme of acceptance. Some people have trouble accepting that they can only lose so much weight without making other sacrifices they are not willing to make. Acceptance works the other way, too. A person might go many years cancer-free, yet have trouble identifying as a cancer survivor or simply as someone who once had cancer but overcame it.

The Power of Perception

The exploration I invite you to take is not simply an intellectual one that involves rational thinking and the conscious mind. It is a journey into the unconscious, where rationality is not the rule. Stories have power, and they are often shaped by our unconscious beliefs and our memories. If we become conscious of our stories and see they are not serving us, we can explore and work with the unconscious influences on them. Then, our self-perceptions are likely to change. For instance, you might identify with being in the prime of your life, only to look in the mirror and be surprised by the signs of aging apparent in your hair, face, and skin. Which should you believe: what the mirror tells you about who you are, or what you feel and believe about who you are? It is your choice, but keep in mind that the consequences of being "unrealistic" or "too optimistic" might be better than you imagine.

Research shows people achieve better health outcomes and enjoy better vitality and health when they have a positive attitude toward aging. Yet so many of us have internalized the story that as we get older, we will experience physical and mental deterioration and lose our relevance. Ellen Langer, PhD, professor of psychology at Harvard University, conducted a "counterclockwise" study in 1979 that showed remarkable results when participants' perceptions of themselves and their vitality were altered. For the duration of the study, men in their late 70s and early 80s spent a week living as if they had traveled back in time 20 years. They temporarily lived in housing where they listened to the music from that earlier era, were surrounded by physical objects from the time, and were encouraged to talk about the events that had occurred back then. Afterward, their mental sharpness, joint flexibility, and appearance (including posture and gait) were compared to those of a control group, and they were found to be sharper, more flexible, and younger-looking than their counterparts.[1] The mind's ability to perceive oneself differently clearly affects the body.

Altering your beliefs about your health can be done not just at the level of the conscious, rational mind but at the level of the unconscious mind, at their source. It is in the unconscious mind that these beliefs are fueled by archetypal energies that determine the themes of your health story.

Impatience is just one example of an energy that can shape your story. It might be fueling a story about your health that could be summed up as, "I can't wait around for others to help me. If it's going to happen, I have to take charge and do things on my own." Impatience could also fuel this story: "I am often impatient but I know how long processes can take, and how long I sometimes have to wait to get answers and help from others. My impatience is a gentle wakeup call to check in with myself to see whether I want to continue to wait and work on my ability to be patient, or take a new action." Identifying the theme of impatience and developing a new relationship with this energy can help you install new beliefs in your unconscious. Themes and energies are so closely related, at least from a Jungian and shamanic perspective, that throughout this book, I will use the terms interchangeably.

Themes, Energies, and Insights

Stories are our way of interpreting our past and current experiences. Writing a new story about what you would like to experience in this moment, and in the months and years to come, means working with energies you can also think of as themes. What is the story about, ultimately? What theme or themes unify your experiences of your health? Perseverance? Irreverence? Playfulness?

In Jungianism, we often look at a story's themes as being powered by archetypes, which may or may not be personified. There are many archetypes, including battling/the warrior, healing/the inner healer, and innocence/the inner child, to name just a few. Archetypes may also be personified as stock characters, such as a wise king or a foolish prince, a comeback kid, or an overworked everyman. They might be thought of as gods or goddesses with the characteristics of those beings—Dionysus, the god of revelry and indulgence, for example, or Hestia, the goddess of hearth and home.

An archetype is a symbolic embodiment of experiences and ideas common to people around the world and across time. Because they have the power to influence our thinking and behavior, archetypes can be thought of as archetypal energies. One of the classic archetypes identified by Jung is the death principle (often personified as the grim reaper). The death principle is an archetype of endings, and its power to influence you could help you to write and bring about a new story.

Let's say a person with a type-A personality and hot temper starts to develop cardiac problems. He might have to let go of the old, confining story called, "If I don't crack the whip, no one will listen, and if I don't do it myself, it won't get done" because anger and impatience can strongly contribute to heart disease. The habit of being aggressive and intimidating may have to go so the person can die to his old self, and so something more helpful and healthy can take the place of these qualities. Death can serve life by energetically removing what is draining you. A gardener prunes away excess branches on a rosebush to allow the life-force of the plant to be directed to the branches with buds that have yet to blossom. After working with the death principle, the type-A person might be able to direct his passion for excellence and drive for productivity more positively rather than expressing it as anger or impatience.

Health is one aspect of your life story that the energy of endings can influence in a positive way. You can use it to let go of shame and disappointment at having lost some of your physical stamina or health, the elasticity of your skin, or the ability to do things you once could do, or had the potential to do, in decades past. The archetypal energy of death can also allow you to let go of fear and anger, emotions responsible for stress that may lead to or exacerbate illness or symptoms of disease. Because this archetypal energy is so important for healing work, I have included an exercise on working with it in Chapter Eight: Revising the Story of Your Health.

Another theme or archetype is the warrior. In folktales, myths, and legends, warriors fight not only for themselves but for their people, for glory, for principle—that is, for something larger than themselves.[2] A cause or purpose can fuel a warrior through the most challenging battles. As you consider your health and physicality, does the archetype of the warrior resonate with you? Are you battling depression, cancer, or your image of yourself as weak and needy? In what ways have you been a warrior, fighting adversarial people or situations, pushing past physical exhaustion because you felt the battle was important? How has that worked for you? Have you fought fruitless battles, or courageously defended yourself against a virus, an infection, or a perception of yourself that was no longer serving you?

You may never have thought about your health in terms of themes, but you may find that in identifying these organizing principles and how they affect you, you gain valuable insights. An excellent way to do that is to combine expanded-awareness practices, which you can use for encountering and working with archetypal energies that animate themes, and an everyday-awareness practice of journaling to explore them further.

The Everyday-Awareness Practice of Journaling

Expanded-awareness practices drawn from shamanic, Jungian, and other traditions can help you to engage energies and access insights and wisdom available to you in your unconscious mind, away from the reach of your conscious, rational, thinking mind. However, I also feel it is important to use journaling to articulate what you have experienced when using these practices, and to record your answers to questions that force you to look within. When journaling, you will probably be in ordinary, everyday awareness, thinking and analyzing, yet you will be drawing on insights you access as a result of using expanded-awareness practices—or even ones you encountered synchronistically.

In a journal, record your health experiences, noting when you are feeling physically fatigued, when pain flares up and what its qualities are, what you ate and did throughout the course of a day, and so forth. Doing so can be helpful for identifying patterns. Expressing your thoughts and emotions on the page can be healing in itself, too, helping you to start writing a new story of your health.

Journal about your experiences with the expanded-awareness practices, too. Ponder these experiences over the course of several days. Come back and reread what you wrote, and allow any new insights to arise. Let your intuition guide you as you interpret what happened when using the practices.

You might feel inspired to investigate a particular topic more thoroughly, or to journal about a memory that suddenly arises or an image that appears in your mind as you write. If so, allow your inner healer time in which to express its wisdom to you, for this aspect of yourself knows what you need to change if you want to experience better health. What looks like a purely physical ailment might be a reflection of something that is happening within you emotionally that you need to address. It is easier to see that when you are thoughtful and reflective instead of in a hurry to figure out the cause of a headache, back pain, or sleepless nights. Your inner healer may tell you that your headache is due to thinking too much about other people's needs and desires instead of focusing on your own.

Beginning to Recognize Your Current Health Story

Initially, as you start to think about how you would describe your story of your health, you might begin to tell a story in which you always play a positive role, patiently managing your health condition and working with your team of healers to reduce bothersome symptoms. Yet you may realize while working with this book and its exercises that your archetypal energy of the dutiful and obedient son or daughter—or the "good girl" or "nice guy"—has sabotaged you in ways you aren't fully conscious of.

It can be tempting to whitewash the story of your health, whether for your benefit or that of others, or both. Many of us tell people "I am fine," or "I'm okay with aging and a few aches and pains," when those are not our true feelings. Saying it makes us believe it, to some degree, but the unconscious knows better. Be honest with yourself about the story of your health right now, as you see it. Begin by doing the following journaling exercise.

JOURNALING EXERCISE: DISCOVER YOUR BELIEFS ABOUT YOUR HEALTH

Circle, underline, or highlight any of the thoughts and beliefs below that resonate with you, or simply identify them and rewrite them in your journal.

- I just want my health to get fixed so I can get back to my old life.
- I don't want to admit I'm afraid of my body aging and becoming unreliable.
- I'm working on improving my health because I've become aware of my limitations and my mortality, and I'm scared.
- My health problems make me less productive, which makes me feel bad about myself.
- I need to improve my health habits but don't know how to make time to attend to my health when I have so much to do and I'm under so much stress.
- I've always been weaker or less agile or less athletic than others.
- I have read studies about nutrition and things people should do for better health, but the experts keep changing their conclusions. I can't keep up, and it bothers me.
- My significant other is worried about my health, and I hate feeling "watched," so I sneak cigarettes, hide my habit of eating junk food, etc.
- I won't baby myself and be a complainer. Stiff upper lip—that's the way I am.
- I don't have time to eat right, get enough sleep, or exercise.

- It's too hard for me to make healthy changes because the people I love and am living with have very different health habits and won't support me in making those changes.
- Cancer runs in my family. I'll probably get it, too.
- I am managing a chronic illness or a serious disease, and I know self-care should be part of my health story, but I forget to take care of myself because I'm always taking care of others.
- I am in a very stressful work or family situation, and I will just have to bear the psychological and physical costs.
- I can't be around people with bad health habits or I'll slip back into my old ways. I don't trust myself to eat right and exercise if I spend time with people who eat poorly and are sedentary.

Add any other statements about your health that are true for you.

Next, look at the list again and identify any themes or emotions you feel match up with these thoughts. Themes are often expressed in one or two words, and they categorize or sum up the story or statement. You will probably identify more than one theme for any particular statement about your health. Here are some examples:

- I just want my health to get fixed so I can get back to my old life. *THEMES: impatience, shortcuts, denial, resistance, rescue*
- I don't want to admit I'm afraid of my body aging and becoming unreliable. *THEMES: endings, fear, shame*
- I'm working on improving my health because I've become aware of my limitations and my mortality, and I'm scared. *THEMES: limitations, scarcity, mortality, fear, taking action*
- My health problems make me less productive, which makes me feel bad about myself. *THEMES: productivity, action, shame, challenges/struggles*
- I need to improve my health habits but don't know how to make time to attend to my health when I have so much to do and I'm under so much stress. *THEMES: lack of time, stress, trouble prioritizing, overworked, overwhelmed, anxious*

Now, take a look at what you have written and see if you can identify a character or familiar plot line you could associate with these thoughts and beliefs and the themes you identified. For instance, you might come up with:

- I just want my health to get fixed so I can get back to my old life. *THEMES: impatience, shortcuts, denial, resistance, rescue. Rushing to get back to where you were instead of exploring the situation. Dorothy in* The Wizard of Oz *wanting to get back home to Kansas. Help me!*
- I don't want to admit I'm afraid of my body aging and becoming unreliable. *THEMES: Endings, fear, shame, not seeing/accepting what is. The foolish old man or the emperor who has no clothes. Searching for the elusive fountain of youth.*
- I'm working on improving my health because I've become aware of my limitations and my mortality, and I'm scared. *THEMES: limitations, scarcity, mortality, fear, taking action. There's never enough time. Time is ticking away. Race against time. Turning back the hands of the clock. Father Time. How do I escape the grim reaper when he comes to the door?*
- My health problems make me less productive, which makes me feel bad about myself. *THEMES: productivity, action, shame, challenges/struggles. "I used to be somebody but I'm not anymore." Washed up. Having to prove my worthiness. Slacker. Sloth. "You can be replaced, you know."*
- I need to improve my health habits but don't know how to make time to attend to my health when I have so much to do and I'm under so much stress. *THEMES: lack of time, stress, trouble prioritizing, overworked, overwhelmed, anxious. The worrywart. The caretaker. Running on empty. No time for myself. I'm last on my list.*

Write in your journal about your responses to this exercise. How did doing it make you feel? What did you learn about your health story?

There are chapters in your health story you can explore in depth using the exercises in this book. These chapters probably have themes associated with them.

Your health story might include chapters on:

- Eating and drinking and weight
- Movement and exercise, flexibility, balance, stamina, and strength
- Sexuality, body image and acceptance, and changes due to midlife hormonal shifts (commonly known as menopause and andropause)
- Management of symptoms of an acute or chronic condition

Within each of these chapters, there is much to explore, including the connections among your physical well-being and your mental and emotional well-being, issues related to aging, bodily systems involved in these chapters, and more.

As you work with individual chapters in your health story, you may decide certain topics are so important to your health story that they deserve their own chapters. However, these four chapters will give you a good start to discovering your story and what you might like to change about it.

Always remember that in the story of your health, everything is interconnected. Your physical experiences, such as weight gain or loss of sexual desire, might be closely related to emotional experiences and beliefs you have not yet explored. You might initially feel a topic within a chapter is not worth exploring, but after doing several exercises in this book, come to realize it is something you want to look at after all.

Certainly, hormonal shifts in midlife may be affecting you more than you realize—and your symptoms management may be related to your eating and drinking habits more than you suspect. For example, many women find their menopausal symptoms of hot flashes and mood swings are reduced when they make simple dietary changes, such as avoiding sugar and alcohol.

Remember, too, that your health story could influence and be influenced by your psychology, your significant relationships, your vocation or employment, your relationship to Source (also known as Spirit, God—and by many other names), and your ways of being of service to others and the planet. Hospitals are devising stress-screening tools so any financial, emotional, or psychological issues that might affect health can be identified.[3]

Many medical professionals are realizing that their patients' health has to be looked at holistically, and that you cannot separate physical symptoms and psychosocial issues. The notion that you can't separate individual consciousness from the matrix affecting all of us is core to holistic medicine, and one that many medical professionals struggle to understand because it is foreign to the medical mind-set. As you do the work of exploring your health story and writing a new and more satisfying one, I encourage you to look at how your health is influenced by other chapters in your life and influences them, too.

While insights may arise as a result of working with expanded-awareness practices to achieve healing, over the years I have come to see that often, people experience healing before they experience understanding.

Maria's story is an example. She has minor neuropathy in both feet. (Neuropathy is a nerve disorder that causes numbness—for her, on the bottoms of her feet, more on the right foot than the left.) Maria used preparatory practices and an expanded-awareness practice called Journey to the Quiet (which you will find later in this book) to see what sort of healing she might experience. The Quiet is a place before creation, where everything exists in potential—a transpersonal realm that has an essence of unconditional love. Her experience was this:

> I opened sacred space by invoking the four directions, Mother Earth, and the Sky Beings. Then I brought in white-gold light to cleanse my energy field. As I envisioned my body's energy field, I perceived my entire right foot as dark and heavy. Mentally, I moved the light through it, pushing the dark energy into the earth, where it was absorbed. I then visualized both feet as normal in color and feeling. I did mindful breathing to relax and enter a deeper state of consciousness.
>
> Next, I visualized going through a tunnel and a beautiful diamond-like crystal grid to the place called the Quiet. This space was completely empty but felt strangely full at the same time, as if it could express itself in form at any moment yet stayed suspended as a void. I asked the Quiet, "What message do you have for me about my health?" After a pause, the answer came: "You need to spend more time in this state." I let the answer penetrate my unconscious, aware that the full meaning was not available to my conscious mind, and waited until I felt it was appropriate to ask, "Is there anything else I need to know?" The response was like an echo: "You need to spend more time here."

I asked the Quiet to take away something I didn't need and should let go of to experience better health. The answer came: sugar cravings. I asked the Quiet to give me something I needed, and soon, a column of white light poured through my eyes into my entire body. It seemed to bring with it resolve to be more disciplined in eating only what my body requires.

After a time, I returned through the crystalline-like structure and the tunnel the way I had come, and closed the sacred space by thanking the six directions. My connection with nature seemed closer, and the experience of feeling the light pour through me seemed especially vivid. Later that day, I noticed that my feet, especially the right one, had more feeling than before, as if the numbness had retreated. Even now, months later, I feel I have less neuropathy than I did before the journey.

Since that experience, I've learned that the message "You need to spend more time here" was helping me see a way to change the neuropathy story that was developing in my body. I recognize now that being in the Quiet gives me a time of absolute stillness to recoup from the stressors in my life, and it allows information from that dimension to flow into my energy field. I believe that aids me in the transformation of consciousness that's going on at a deeper level. It's amazing to see how much information can get transmitted in a fraction of time.

Your experience of the Quiet might be somewhat different from Maria's. For example, you might not get a visual image as you are traveling there or once you arrive in this place. Some might say these places and experiences are imaginary and a product of the unconscious influencing your cognitions and impressions. I leave it for you to decide.

The Contents of Your Unconscious Mind

The expanded-awareness practices in this book engage the non-rational part of your brain, which is involved in your experience of the unconscious. Know that what is in your unconscious is hidden from your conscious, rational mind. Expanding your awareness is a way to bring what's hidden into the light of your consciousness. In your unconscious, you can find hidden beliefs such as "I need to be sick to get attention from other people" or "I'm naturally going to lose my flexibility and strength as I age, and there's not much I can do about it." You can also find insights and archetypal energies helpful for eliminating or altering these hidden beliefs. To access these energies and alter their influence on your health story, you must reduce the activity of the conscious mind, which hides what is in the unconscious.

Some of these insights and energies transcend the limitations of individual consciousness and unconsciousness and are found in what Carl Jung called the collective unconscious, as I mentioned earlier. You will be working with your unconscious to better understand how your hidden thoughts and emotions may be affecting your physical health.

Perhaps the best way to describe the value of the expanded-awareness practices in this book is simply this: You access hidden information from the unmanifest realms and make sense of it through embodiment (feeling things in your body) or intuition. You can ask for and receive the help of archetypal energies—assistance in better understanding what you are experiencing, for bringing to light insights that are hidden from your conscious mind, and for self-healing. You can call forth these energies through using the practices and working with the energies and insights you encounter.

As you learn that your own stories have been enacted by others, and have universal qualities, you will gain a new perspective on your health and well-being. You will contextualize them, putting them into a larger story of your life as one individual who is part of the human experience on Earth. You will realize you are not alone, that experiencing ebbs and flows is natural, and that birth, growth, aging, and death are part of life. In turn, these insights will help you to not just write but live according to a better and more satisfying health story.

CHAPTER TWO

Consciousness, Energy, and the Body

As you explore your health story, it will soon become clear that energy, feelings, and thoughts, both conscious and unconscious, are intertwined and can influence your physical health. For example, anxiety can cause heart arrhythmia and hyperventilation, while heart arrhythmia from atrial fibrillation can cause anxiety. Everything is interconnected within the matrix, the larger energy field we are all a part of and woven into energetically, and which is hidden from the conscious mind.

At the core of energy medicine, including shamanic approaches to healing, is the idea that there are energy fields surrounding and pervading the physical body, and that by working with these fields, you can improve your health and your body's functioning.

You might think of the physical body as encased by a mental/emotional body, which in turn is encased by a soul body and, beyond that, a luminous energy body—each body stacked like Russian nesting dolls, one within the other. Energetic messages and archetypal energies present in the matrix may travel through a person's luminous energy body to affect emotions and thoughts as well as cells, tissues, and organs.

If it seems strange to think of your physical body as being encased by what could be called your mind, which is associated with thoughts and emotions, it's probably because most of us were taught that we experience these things within the brain. What if the mind, or personal consciousness, is not contained within this vital organ but instead surrounds it, influencing it? Entertain this concept for now so that you can better understand how shamanic and Jungian traditions might mesh together and even fit well with other traditions, such as the notion of chakras (more on that shortly).

Science shows us that when we experience thoughts and feelings, areas in the brain associated with them are more active. You can observe that a person is feeling emotions if you look at a brain scan performed with an MRI (magnetic resonance imaging) machine because the emotional activity is both chemical and electromagnetic in nature. You might not be able to determine exactly what emotion that person is feeling, or what thoughts the emotion is connected to, however.

One way to think of thoughts and feelings is to imagine them as being energetic in nature and encoded with information. The thought and the feeling are often intertwined. Let's say you experience pleasure as you have the fleeting thought "I love eating chocolate." The pleasurable sensation is associated with a rush of the neurotransmitter dopamine. Your brain's experience of feeling and thinking about pleasure can be detected on an MRI. Although thoughts and feelings are associated with the mind, and therefore the brain, you might also say they are experienced energetically throughout the body and associated with hormones and neurotransmitters produced in the brain (and, in the case of serotonin, in the digestive system as well).

We speak of being happy right down to our toes or having a warm feeling in our heart. Such sayings reflect our awareness that emotions are not simply experienced biochemically in the brain. In fact, emotional stress can lead to excess stomach acid being released, causing a sensation of nausea experienced in the head and in the belly. This possibility is acknowledged in idiomatic expressions such as "I can't stomach this confrontation."

Emotional stressors, such as thoughts that generate feelings of fear and anger, can cause muscle tension in the neck or elsewhere in the body. Massage therapists will often say to a client, "Where in your body do you hold your tension?" Conceivably, you could be holding specific emotions, such as grief or anger, in a particular area of your body, too.

Shamanic practices work with removing and replacing the energy of these emotions. The shaman observes the disturbance in the energy field, removes energetic blockages, and brings healing energy into the empty space. This type of balancing work mirrors the idea of removing toxins from the body and replenishing it with healthy foods. Removing an emotional stressor from your life and bringing in an emotionally replenishing habit might balance your energy and lead to physical healing.

What happens if we skip removing something energetically and simply try to bring in healing? Once, during a shamanic ceremony I participated in, my intent was to bring in the universal light, the creative light energy from the Quiet. During the ceremony, I realized it was a battle to clear myself and get rid of the things I needed to get rid of energetically in order to have room for that light to enter into. I was aware of how difficult it was for me to clear blockages and create an opening for the light. So while I was eager to bring in healing light, I had to admit that the shamanic notion of an exchange of energies—taking something out before putting something in—had validity for me. See whether it has validity for you as you work with the practices in this book.

Be open to the notions of energy bodies and mental, emotional, and energetic influences on your health. They explain a lot about why energy medicine—and Jungian and shamanic techniques—seem to work.

Energetic Influences on Health:
A Shamanic View

According to the shamanic worldview, illness and disease manifest first in the luminous energy body that surrounds and interpenetrates a person's physical body. This luminous energy body, or field, is affected by myriad forces, including forces in the matrix.

Beliefs and emotions we experience also affect the luminous energy body surrounding the mental/emotional body. When that happens, the luminous energy body can develop imbalances and areas of disturbed, stale, heavy, or dark energy that in turn may affect the mental/emotional body and even the physical body. A shaman would say that if you were to heal an illness but did not deal with the disturbance in your energy field that created the illness, your ailment would be likely to return. The damage in the largest Russian nesting doll affects the dolls within it.

Monitoring your thoughts and emotions can alert you to a disturbance in your energy field, which you can heal by using shamanic techniques to clear it. In theory, that might prevent an ailment, reduce its intensity, promote physical healing, or improve your immunity.

Can you imagine that an imbalance in your luminous energy body is causing both emotional and physical symptoms? We know that a toxic electromagnetic signal—radiation, x-rays, and the like—can affect your body's own electromagnetic field, enter your body, and affect your cells and even your DNA. That in turn can make you more prone to disease at the physical or psychological levels. We also know that information comes into your body embedded in energy. Perhaps archetypal energies with particular qualities, such as nurturance or playfulness, could affect cells and DNA. If such energies travel from your energy body into your physical body and switch on the genes that prevent illness rather than the ones that give birth to disease, it would be good to know more about such a mechanism and how to work with it effectively.

The Personal Energy Body and the Chakras

One possible explanation for how the energy field affects the body, and vice versa, is that our physical, mental, and emotional experiences affect our chakras. In Hindu and yogic traditions, it is said that a number of energy centers, or chakras, are woven into the body's energy field. Chakras receive, transform, and transmit energies. Imbalances in the chakras can lead to illness. Therefore, techniques to cleanse and balance your luminous body, chakras, and your physical body's energetic pathways are important.

Like many shamans around the world, as well as many energy medicine healers, I recognize not only the luminous body but chakras. Based on my experiences, I believe that when we work with the chakras for the sake of healing, we are working with energy that affects the body.

Shaped like funnels or vortexes, chakras have narrow ends said to reach into the physical body at points along the spine while their wide ends face outward. Chakras spin in a clockwise direction (that is, if the clock were resting on your body and the face was facing outward). When chakras are clogged with dark, heavy energies, their movement is impeded. They slow down or spin in a counterclockwise direction as they try to clear what they need to clear—a process you can help with when you do a chakra cleansing practice (you'll find one later in this book).

In Hindu tradition, which has become popular in America, there are seven chakras.[1]

- **The first chakra**, located in the groin at the base of the spine, associated with the kundalini, or life force energy, as well as security, safety, and a person's connection to the earth
- **The second chakra**, located in the sacrum area below the navel, associated with the spleen, the pelvic bowl, and the genitals, sexuality, generative powers, and creative expression

- **The third chakra**, located in the middle of the torso just below the ribs at the solar plexus, and associated with digestion as well as personal power
- **The fourth chakra**, located in the center of the breast near the heart, associated with this vital organ and with love and relationships
- **The fifth chakra**, located at the throat and associated with the throat and thyroid gland, communication, and speaking one's truth
- **The sixth chakra**, located at the forehead between the eyebrows, associated with the "third eye" of spiritual insight and wisdom
- **The seventh chakra**, located at the top of the head or crown, associated with the pineal gland and one's connection to Spirit or Source

Chakras are said to correspond to the physical body and organs, and to have symbolic meanings. Some believe each chakra also corresponds to a certain set of emotional and psychological issues. For example, some have suggested that an imbalance in the fifth chakra—which hinders it from freely spinning in a clockwise direction—causes, or is associated with, a tendency to "swallow" emotions and opinions someone is afraid to express. The idea is that these emotional problems could be manifesting as physical problems in the throat area and producing symptoms such as a sore throat, difficulty swallowing, raspiness, nodes on the vocal cords, or a problem with the thyroid (a gland located in the throat).

You might find it helpful to explore these correspondences, and to think about the chakras or their associations metaphorically as you work through this book. Chakra healing is a type of energy medicine that fits well with shamanic and Jungian healing modalities. (In Chapter Eight: Revising the Story of Your Health, you will find a chakra-cleansing practice that will help you cleanse your energy field.)

From the Outside In and the Inside Out

While your energy field can affect your body, according to shamanism and the chakra healing tradition as well as other energy medicine traditions, physical disturbances can also affect your emotional/mental body and your soul—at least, this is what I believe based on my work and experiences.

If you have ever cut into a bruised apple, you might have realized the external bruise had affected the inner flesh—but you might also have noticed rot from within that had not yet made its way outward to the skin of the fruit. So, for example, a person with Lyme disease contracted from the bite of a tick will experience fatigue of physical origin. However, emotional fatigue can set in as well, along with mental fatigue from trying to manage a challenging health condition.

Perhaps the individual will develop depression, which combined with mental fatigue could, conceivably, lead to a disturbance in the energy body layer that I am calling the soul. The chakras might become clogged with heavy, dense energy that slows their spinning and might even cause them to spin counterclockwise instead of the usual clockwise direction.

In sum, by addressing the disturbance within—perhaps at the level of your blood or organs, or perhaps at a cellular level—I believe you might be able to prevent a disturbance within from growing and affecting other layers of your energy bodies.

Unconscious and Energetic Influences on the Body

Jungian psychological techniques are not part of energy medicine per se, but they do involve consciousness and energies. In her book *The Psyche of the Body,* Jungian analyst Denise Gimenez Ramos writes, "The psyche induces somatization of those conflicted and traumatic situations that could not be integrated on the conscious plane."[2]

We all know that unresolved conflicts and unhealed wounds from trauma can affect us psychologically, but not everyone is aware of how they can affect us physically—and often, symbolically. Jungians say that to deal with psychological processes that cause psychosomatic illness, we must work with archetypal energies, such as those we experience as symbols and inner figures.

Ramos tells the story of Beth, a patient with rheumatoid arthritis and its common symptoms of inflamed, painful, stiff joints. Using Jungian techniques and interactions with symbols to explore and address what was hidden in her unconscious, Beth freed herself to begin expressing more anger toward her husband instead of repressing it. She also became less rigid in her habits and beliefs regarding cleanliness and order.

Additionally, she found physical relief from symptoms of her autoimmune disorder, and the stiffness and immobility of her joints that had not responded to homeopathy or acupuncture were reduced. Prior to undergoing Jungian analysis, Beth had found her power in stoicism, in quietly accepting her life as it was rather than working to improve her unhappy relationship with her husband. "We might note that the inflamed joints revealed the 'inflamed psyche,' her silent revolt against the constant violation of her essence," Ramos writes.[3]

Similarly, a woman I worked with began using Jungian techniques—as well as shamanic ones—to interact with symbols and their archetypal energies. She came to recognize that her stiff neck was related to her feeling judged, and soon came to realize she was judging others as well. As she began to change these emotional patterns, using several of the techniques for healing I present to you in this book, the stiffness in her neck eased, even though there was no physiological explanation for this to happen. I believe this is another case of the potential for altering our beliefs and emotions by working with our health stories' themes and their archetypal energies differently.

Jungians identify a personal unconscious and the collective unconscious. Within the collective unconscious reside archetypes including the ego, the persona (the mask we present to the world), the shadow (the aspect of consciousness we deny because it makes us uncomfortable), and the anima and animus (inner feminine and masculine aspects of self), as well as others.

Archetypes have universal qualities, which is why we see similar themes and similar gods, goddesses, and myths in many human cultures. When you work with an archetypal energy—for example, ordinariness—it might take the form of an inner figure such as an everyday, nondescript bureaucrat, or an ordinary animal such as a gray pigeon or squirrel (if those are common animals in your environment). You might encounter a symbolic representation of ordinariness, such as a scoop of vanilla ice cream.

These symbols may have much to tell you about your feeling of being ordinary. For example, let's say you live according to a story in which you are ordinary, nothing special, and not deserving of any more than what you have. This might cause you to feel unworthy of better health and to work with healers who are inattentive toward you.

The archetypal energies Jungians identify are distinct from energies such as the electromagnetic field of the earth, or the energy inherent in the ultraviolet rays beaming down to us from the sun. However, you could also say that the earth is a symbol corresponding to an archetypal energy associated with the qualities of earth, and that the sun is an archetypal energy as well as a symbol one finds in many cultures, religions, and spiritual traditions.

How would you work with an archetypal energy affecting your health story? Let's say you realize that the archetypal energy of an innocent child is benefitting you. It helps you to be playful, lighthearted, and less stressed. Then again, you might find it has negative aspects—or what Jungians call shadow qualities. Perhaps the innocent child energy causes you to be gullible and too trusting of others and their advice.

This archetypal energy might be able to teach you about being open and trusting yet better able to listen to your instincts and value your own ideas about improving your health. You could work with the innocent child energy by engaging it as an archetype within the unconscious and dialoguing with it, asking questions and listening to its answers, which may come to you symbolically or as an understanding, a sensation, or words.

Jung wrote that the collective unconscious exists within all of us individually and collectively. This can be a difficult concept to grasp if you are thinking in terms of ordinary reality and how things relate to one another. How can all the thoughts and feelings shared by human beings exist within us? But the collective unconscious can also be thought of as a field of energy, or the matrix, or a collection of transpersonal realms. Shamans would say that when we journey, altering our consciousness and reducing the influence of the individual consciousness that identifies with the body, we can access information and insights from the past, present, and future. We can see alternative outcomes for ourselves and how we might achieve them. We might gain deeper understanding of our past or present and integrate aspects of ourselves we have lost or forgotten and which can serve us in writing a new story.

As you become open to the possibility of working with your own unconscious, you gain access to even greater insights and to many helpful energies. Jungians would say these exist in the collective unconscious. And shamans would say they are available in transpersonal realms, such as the lower world or upper world.

In such realms, you might find the answers to questions such as, "What do I need to do to regain my vitality?" "Is this treatment working for me, and should I continue it?" "What is triggering my fatigue?" and "What will happen if I continue on my present course, making no changes to my lifestyle habits?" The answers might surprise you.

Once you have accessed information and energies that were formerly hidden from you, a new story of your health is more likely to come into being instead of remaining a mere wish list. You may discover underlying causes of illness and disease you can now address. It is one thing to say, "I am going to reverse this condition," and another thing entirely to believe at the deepest level that this is possible. The new story you write for your health may not take hold if you aren't aware of any unconscious beliefs that are sabotaging it, such as a belief that the only way to address a particular physical ailment is through undergoing a certain medical procedure.

Although it might be hard to believe, perhaps you can beat the odds or reverse a health condition by working with the unconscious. The prognosis your doctors give you might be grim, and yet intellectually, you know some people have achieved so-called miracle healings. Be open to possibilities for your health that may contradict what you think of as the most likely outcome.

What It Means to "Heal"

Healing can take many forms. For a cancer patient to heal, a physician might prescribe radiation, surgery, chemotherapy, a change in diet, and rest. But the patient might also need to talk about the experience and find meaning in it. To "heal" might require that the individual begin to understand how the cancer fits into his soul's journey. It might involve a commitment to changing his attitudes and priorities. Finally, healing might involve clearing and balancing at the energetic level and establishing a new or renewed relationship with Source.

From a spiritual perspective, in which the soul's experiences and development are paramount, "healing" might occur even if the patient dies of cancer. However, in doing the healing work, the patient is likely to maximize the possibility of recovery. Recovery might include improved physical health as well as writing and living according to a new story that supports it—including a new health story.

In the next chapter, you will start the process of writing a new and better story of your health, and bringing it to life by identifying your current story.

CHAPTER THREE

What Is the Current Story of Your Health?

When someone asks, "How are you?" do you reflexively say, "I'm okay" or "I'm fine … and you?" rather than taking a moment to think about how you really feel? To make changes in your health story, you have to be willing to be scrupulously honest with yourself about what your health story is currently, even if you don't tell others about your health concerns.

By closely examining your current health story, you will begin to see how elements in it interrelate—diet, exercise regimen, stress management, and symptoms of aging or chronic conditions. Then it will be easier to be truthful with yourself and with your health care providers and any loved ones who support you in being healthy and active. Denial leads to worse problems down the road.

If you are reading this book, you probably feel you have to change your health story to some degree. However, your conscious mind may deny how much potential there is for transformation and what will happen if you do not access that potential. As emotionally challenging as it may be to face what your unconscious mind knows, using expanded-awareness practices can alert you to important truths your conscious mind is avoiding. Being dishonest with yourself will hurt you in the long run.

In this chapter, you will find many questions to answer in a journal. Remember that it is also important to journal about your experiences after using the expanded-awareness practices in this book. Begin by working with the rational, analytical brain and simply answering the questions here. They will take some thought and reflection, and you may wish to break up the work rather than try to do it all at once. I think it is a good idea to spend several hours working with these questions before you begin to use the expanded-awareness practices for tapping into the deep wisdom of your unconscious. The combination of journaling and expanded-awareness practices will make it easier for you to identify and understand your health story to date as well as to begin writing a new, more satisfying one.

Despite your efforts to make changes at the margins—altering your habits in simple ways to bring about better health—you might find you can't stick to your goals. In that case, you might journey to the lower world to gain insights and energies to better understand any hidden resistance to changing your habits. You might decide to dialogue with your resistance, or a symbol or inner figure you encountered during your journey, to learn more about why it is so hard for you to stop eating late at night, follow your physicians' orders, or exercise regularly. Also, you might want to begin working with these journaling questions, take a break, and come back to finish them after you have read the entire book; you will find more expanded-awareness practices in later chapters.

As you work with the questions here, you may want to focus first on the most problematic aspects of your health rather than working through the chapters in the order I have laid out. If you choose to do this, I encourage you to complete the exercises anyway, even the ones on topics you presently do not have concerns about. Often, we are not aware of dissatisfying aspects of our health stories until we peer more closely into specific chapters we might have thought to be relatively unimportant, given our most pressing health concerns, such as pain or physical limitations. As you answer the questions in this chapter, you may start to recognize symptoms and signs of developing problems you need to address.

Writing Out the Current Story of Your Health

To identify the story of your health—the one that you tell yourself—you can start simply by writing it in a few paragraphs or a few pages. However, before you begin, there are some things you should know about this process.

First, I suggest you use a personal journal to write the story of your health and to record your answers to the questions in this book, as well as your impressions after having used the expanded-awareness practices. Understanding what you experienced or why you felt better after using an exercise may come later. In rereading your journal, you might find you have even deeper insights.

Second, keep in mind that we tend to focus on problems and not health itself, and we often forget about what is working in our health story. When you are writing it out, make sure you do not focus too much on the negative, ignoring the positive.

Third, know that looking at the bigger story of your health rather than simply considering what you know you would like to change or fix makes it easier to feel grateful for the aspects of your health that are excellent. Gratitude can give you perspective that helps you to believe you have the power to improve your health. I have buildup of plaque in my arteries, which is distressing, but I also can say I am not in pain and I have good stamina. When I start to think pessimistically about having to make doctors' appointments, take medication, manage my discomfort, or otherwise address my health challenges, it helps to remember what is working about my health story.

Fourth, begin writing your earliest memories of experiencing your body—its strengths, its weaknesses, and its mysteries and pleasures. Or, you might start with adolescence, a time when many people first begin to think about their bodies. You might begin with a strong memory of when your attention was drawn to your body—a serious illness, an accident, or a significant transformation in the state of your health or your physical experience.

If violent acts have caused changes in how you relate to your body, be especially careful to pay attention to your emotions as you write this story. In fact, you may wish to write your health story with a therapist's guidance and support or discuss it with your therapist after you have written it.

As you write your story, whether it starts with your earliest memories of your health and is linear, or you begin at an important point in your tale and skip around to write about different points in your life as you tell it, remember to go back to your experience of your physicality and health before you began to have problems. Identify both what is not working in the story of your health and what is. Write about any positive experiences you had after you began to develop a disease or condition, started to age, or felt the effects of the hormonal changes associated with menopause or andropause. For example, you may come to realize that after developing your health condition, you became more aware of your need to reduce stress that can bring on symptoms. Perhaps you made changes in your life to avoid emotional agitation.

Once you have finished writing the story of your health, you can look at it even more closely by working with specific aspects of it—its chapters, so to speak. Also, keep in mind as you answer the questions below that they are the details in a larger story of your health and your life.

Consider the "Chapters" in the Story of Your Health

The following is a list of chapters in the story of your health that I think you might benefit from exploring. Were these chapters a part of the story of your health that you just wrote? If you did not write about them, is that because you are uncomfortable thinking about them?

You might have other chapters to your health story besides the ones I have identified and created questions around. If you can think of any other chapters, add them to this list and ponder them as you write in your journal and you identify the story of your health.

1. *Eating, drinking, and weight*
2. *Movement and exercise, flexibility, strength, balance, and stamina*
3. *Sexuality, body image and body acceptance, issues regarding menopause or andropause (sexual and hormonal changes in midlife)*
4. *Symptoms management for various chronic health conditions, or addressing the occasional acute ailment*

As you do the journaling work in this chapter, think about the themes you have already identified, and how they have influenced these specific aspects of your health. And again, after you use the expanded-awareness practices, be sure to journal about your experiences to gain further insights.

CHAPTER 1: Eating, Drinking, and Weight

- **What works/good habits.** When it comes to eating, drinking, and weight, which habits are working for you and which aren't? What might you do to improve your habits?
- **Origin of challenges.** What is contributing to any problems you are encountering with this aspect of your health? When did you begin developing habits that aren't working for you now? What else was going on in your life at the time?
- **Connections.** Do you see any connections among your eating,

drinking, and weight and other areas of your health? For example, when you are giving in to bad habits, do you also experience problems with mood, stamina, pain, or management of a chronic ailment? Do you understand those connections?

- **Being informed.** Are there steps you could take today to get better information regarding this chapter of your health—and if so, what are they?

- **Partnering.** Can you identify a professional who can partner with you in changing this chapter in the story of your health, such as a physician or nutritionist? Do you have support from people around you—such as family, friends, or members of a support group—who can help you address your issues in this chapter?

    For example, does your spouse support you in losing weight, or in changing how you eat? Could you find a weight-loss partner who can help you be accountable to your goals for changing your eating habits and losing weight? Would it help to join a support group such as Weight Watchers, Overeaters Anonymous, or Alcoholics Anonymous? Would it help to cook with others, or take gardening or cooking classes with others, to get support for developing new eating habits?

- **Genetics and family history.** How have your genetics or family legacy influenced your thinking about eating and drinking? For example, do you hold beliefs such as "We're all overweight in my family, and there's not much I can do about it," or "No matter what I eat or drink, I'm destined to die young because of my genetics"?

- **Stress.** What is the role of stress in your chapter on eating, drinking, and weight? How might you reduce your stress to improve this chapter of your health?

- **Goals.** What, if any, goals do you have regarding eating, drinking, and weight? Why did you choose these goals?

- **Payoffs to resisting change vs. payoffs to change.** What are the payoffs to continuing your unhealthy and problematic eating and drinking habits, if any? Can you imagine finding another way to achieve those payoffs? For example, if you feel empowered by the freedom to choose unhealthy foods whenever you want to indulge your cravings, could you find another way to achieve your goal of feeling empowered? Are there payoffs to change that you are missing out on? If so, what are they?

- **Identifying themes.** Can you identify some themes that are influencing this chapter in your health story? If you have digestive problems, what are all the ways in which you are not "digesting well" in your life? If food moves through you too quickly, are there other things that nourish you in some way but which move through your life too quickly, keeping you from absorbing all their nourishment? If you are not eliminating well because of gastrointestinal issues, is that a metaphor for being constipated in some way? Consider what your health problems around eating, drinking, and weight mean for you metaphorically.
- **Your chapter's title.** Is there a saying, or song, book, or movie title, that summarizes what you are experiencing in regard to this aspect of your health? For example, could this chapter of your health story be titled, "Eat, drink, and be merry, for tomorrow you die," "Carrying the weight of the world," "Sweets for the sweet," "I deserve it, I earned it, I'm eating it!" "What's right is right and what's left—I'll eat!" "Moderation in all things," "Paying for past sins," or something else?
- **Concerns about mortality.** Does this chapter in your health story cause you to worry about your mortality? If so, why? As we age, our metabolism changes, and weight gain often serves as a physical reminder that time is passing and we are growing older. Consider whether this is an issue for you.

If you are confused by conflicting information about what to eat and which nutritional supplements, if any, you should take, you might want to consider what you can do about that. Author and healthy eating advocate Michael Pollan has wise advice: "Eat food. Not too much. Mostly plants." [1] When it comes to weight, government numbers regarding a healthy weight have changed over the years. There is controversy about whether these numbers are too low or should not be given as much attention as we give other facets of health. Also, recently, medical experts have called into question the value of the body mass index (BMI), which is calculated based on your height and weight, as an indicator of health.

As you work with each of the four chapters in the story of your health, you may wish to do research before trying to set goals and rewrite it. You might be surprised by how much health recommendations have changed over the years. Also, your body's needs might be different. Tuning in to how you feel and whether you have any unpleasant symptoms when you consume certain foods or beverages can be a good guide to whether or not to stick with a particular type of diet.

CHAPTER 2: Movement and Exercise, Flexibility, Strength, Balance, and Stamina

- **What works/good habits.** When it comes to movement and exercise, flexibility, strength, balance, and stamina, which habits are working for you and which aren't? What might you do to improve your habits?
- **Origin of challenges.** What is contributing to any problems you are encountering with this aspect of your health? When did you begin developing these habits that aren't working for you now (such as living a sedentary lifestyle)? What else was going on in your life at the time?
- **Connections.** Do you see any connections among your movement and exercise, flexibility, strength, balance, and stamina and other areas of your health? For example, when you are giving in to bad habits, do you also experience problems with mood, pain, or management of a chronic ailment? Do you understand those connections?
- **Being informed.** Are there steps you could take today to get better information regarding this chapter of your health? If so, what are they?
- **Partnering.** Can you identify a professional who can partner with you in changing this chapter in the story of your health, such as a physician, personal trainer, or physical therapist? Do you have support from people around you—such as family, friends, or members of a support group—who can help you address your issues in this chapter? For example, could a friend be an exercise partner who helps you be accountable to your goals? Does your workplace support you in getting more movement throughout the day?
- **Genetics and family history.** How have your genetics or family legacy influenced your thinking about movement and exercise? For example, do you hold beliefs such as, "In my family, we are too intellectual to care about something so ordinary or boring as exercise or sports" or "Competition is what makes the game fun"? Do you have a story such as, "My relatives tend to be weak and asthmatic, and so am I"?
- **Stress.** What is the role of stress in this chapter of your health story? How might you reduce your stress to improve this chapter?

- **Goals.** What, if any, goals do you have regarding movement and exercise? Flexibility? Balance? Strength? Stamina? Why did you choose those goals?
- **Payoffs to resisting change vs. payoffs to change.** Are there any emotional payoffs to not making changes in this chapter of your health story? What are they? Can you imagine finding another way to achieve those payoffs? For example, if you enjoy a particular activity that is sedentary, could you enjoy it and get movement at the same time? Could you find a form of exercise that you enjoy so much you even look forward to exercising, one that makes you feel good in your body and confident, that gets you out into nature, or that helps you to socialize? Are there payoffs to change that you are missing out on, and if so, what are they?
- **Identifying themes.** Can you identify some themes that are influencing this chapter in your health story? Are there ways in which you have become inflexible emotionally, physically, or mentally, making "inflexibility" a theme in your health story and possibly your overall story, too? Are you balanced in your thoughts, seeing multiple sides of an issue, or in your emotions? How does stamina or endurance express itself in other areas of your life? Do you "hang in there" or quit too easily? How does your strength express itself? Are you too strong in some ways, too weak in others, or appropriately strong?
- **Your chapter's title.** Is there a saying, or song, book, or movie title, that summarizes what you are experiencing in regard to this aspect of your health? For example, would you say, "Keep on keeping on, no matter the cost," "I'm slowing down," "My bones are tired, and I am weary," "Tired of running but afraid to stop and rest," or "If you can't do it well, don't do it at all?"
- **Concerns about mortality.** Does this chapter in your story of your health cause you to worry about your mortality? If so, why? Flexibility, balance, strength, and stamina tend to be reduced as part of the aging process, and they are often lost to some degree when you have a medical condition or disease. You might have to work harder to maintain them or bring them back, and this change can serve as a physical reminder that you will not live forever. Consider whether your mortality is weighing on your mind and heart.

If you used to be able to engage in a certain type of exercise, such as playing tennis or jogging, but no longer can without risking injury or experiencing pain, this may be difficult for you to accept. Identifying as an athlete, or as someone who is "physically fit," can prevent you from finding ways to get healthy exercise that do not fit in with your old story. You might have been socializing, flirting, looking good, and getting multiple benefits from being a runner, and when you stopped being able to run, you may have lost all of these. You might need a new story of your health that will incorporate getting movement and exercise in ways that work for you now, given any limitations you have.

Olivia, one of my workshop participants, journeyed to learn more about how to overcome the gastrointestinal problems she was having (as noted earlier, a journey is an expanded-awareness practice you will use that has its origins in shamanism). Olivia learned that she needed to let go of competitive rowing, an activity she had enjoyed for many years. By dialoguing with symbols and figures she encountered, she discovered that she was taking competitive rowing too seriously, and the stress created by her need to win was contributing to her gastrointestinal issues. She also realized she was competitive in other areas of her life and this pattern was not serving her as well as she thought it was. Olivia further dialogued with her competitiveness, and ended up feeling less concerned about whether she won or lost. After becoming more aware of the stress she was creating for herself, Olivia found she was able to let go of these self-generated pressures and enjoy rowing without taking it so seriously. Her gastrointestinal health much improved.

Many people may find this chapter of their health story is difficult to address because they have jobs that require them to spend much of the day sitting. According to the *Wall Street Journal*, "Studies have found that sedentary behavior, including sitting for extended periods, increases the risk for developing dozens of chronic conditions, from cancer and diabetes to cardiovascular disease and nonalcoholic fatty liver disease." [2] Over time, too much sitting and a lack of adequate exercise can both take a toll on physical health.[3] Repetitive stress injuries and deterioration of the neck and spine due to sitting all day are two examples. In the new health story you will write, you might want to address this topic.

If you are experiencing minor aches and pains due to the way you move, think beyond "I need to get exercise to be healthy." Exploring the themes of movement and exercise can help you gain insights and make changes you might not realize you should make when you simply think of movement as "working out." Even just walking, stretching, or doing light physical activity can reduce your risk of health problems, as can changing your posture often if you have to sit much of the day.[4] In addition, you might want to try devices that can help you get exercise while you work, such as under-the-desk pedaling machines, standing desks, and treadmill desks.

There are many pleasurable ways of getting movement that contribute to flexibility, strength, balance, and stamina, as well as overall health. Walking, hiking, stretching, doing yoga, tai chi, and qigong, dancing, and other activities often involve very little preparation and can also help you to get exercise in ways that are social and not costly. If you have a serious illness, or are recovering from an injury, these activities, which are often gentle, may help you not only get healthy movement but also improve your mood. If you're experiencing stiff or inflexible joints and ligaments, or have poor balance or little strength and stamina, you might want to look closely at how much sitting you do, and whether you need to do different types of exercise and movement to improve in these areas.

Also, we are seeing research into the connections between movement and exercise and the natural world, whether it is walking in the woods as opposed to on a city street, or taking advantage of natural sunlight as part of your daily routine that includes exercise. Books such as *Blue Mind* and *Your Brain on Nature* have explored these connections among nature, well-being, exercise and movement, and health—particularly in regard to lower blood levels of the stress hormone cortisol, an outcome associated with improved mood and greater immunity. The human body evolved within nature, so it makes sense that you might experience better health if you not only get movement but also do it in natural settings.

CHAPTER 3: Sexuality, Body Acceptance and Body Image, Issues regarding Menopause or Andropause (Sexual and Hormonal Changes in Midlife)

- **What works/good habits.** When it comes to sexuality, body acceptance and body image, and issues regarding sexual and hormonal changes in midlife, which habits are working for you and which habits aren't? What might you do to improve your habits?
- **Origin of challenges.** What is contributing to any problems you are

encountering with this aspect of your health? When did you begin developing the habits that aren't working for you now?

For example, if you are no longer having and enjoying sex, but once did, when did the change happen, and what else was going on in your life at the time?

- **Connections.** How is the type of sexual expression you are able to participate in affecting your body image and body acceptance, and vice versa? How are the hormonal changes of midlife affecting your experience of your sexuality, or your body image and body acceptance, if at all? Do you need to make changes to be more satisfied and self-accepting? Do you see any connections between this chapter of your health story and any other chapters?

   For example, when you are having problems in this area of your health, do you also experience seemingly unrelated problems, such as with eating and drinking habits, weight, or movement and exercise? With stress, mood, or pain? Do you wrestle with issues of mortality when you are experiencing problems with this chapter? When this area of your health is satisfying to you, do problems in another chapter or aspect of your health story get reduced or even disappear?

- **Being informed.** Are there steps you could take today to get better information regarding this chapter of your health—and if so, what are they?

- **Partnering.** Can you identify a professional who can partner with you in changing this chapter in the story of your health, such as a physician or therapist? Do you have support from people around you—such as family, friends, or members of a support group—who could help you address your issues in this chapter? For example, does your sexual/romantic partner support you in changing this chapter of your health story to be more satisfying to you?

- **Genetics and family history.** How have your genetics or family legacy influenced your thinking about your sexuality, body image and acceptance, or hormonal changes in midlife? For example, do you hold beliefs such as "In my family, the women get old, fat, and unhappy after menopause," "My family taught me it was vain to think much about my body and its appearance," "In my family, we don't talk about sexuality, much less sexual dysfunction or dissatisfaction or sexual preferences," or "I am afraid that my sexual feelings are changing and wonder what that means for me and how I will be seen by my family"?

- **Stress.** What is the role of stress in this chapter in your health story? How might you reduce your stress to improve this chapter?
- **Goals.** What, if any, goals do you have with respect to experiencing and expressing your sexuality? Body image and body acceptance? Managing the hormonal shifts of midlife? Why did you choose those goals?
- **Payoffs to resisting change vs. payoffs to change.** What, if any, payoffs are there to not addressing the issues in this chapter in the story of your health?

    For example, if you were to increase your sexual desire, or change the way you express your sexuality, would there be unpleasant consequences? Are there ways to make expressing your sexuality more pleasurable that could help you enjoy your sexuality more? And if so, what are they? Are there payoffs to addressing your beliefs and feelings about your own attractiveness, such as gaining more confidence overall or feeling better about who you are? Are there payoffs to change that you are missing out on? And if so, what are they?

- **Identifying themes.** Can you identify some themes that are influencing this chapter in your health story? Are you struggling to regain a sense of virility or womanliness that you have lost? Have you lost your fertility or potency, figuratively speaking? Do you feel you are experiencing a midlife shift?
- **Your chapter's title.** Is there a saying, or song, book, or movie title, that summarizes what you are experiencing in regard to this aspect of your health? For example, would you say, "I need sexual healing," "over the hill," or "past my prime"?
- **Concerns about mortality.** Does this chapter in your story of your health cause you to worry about your mortality? If so, why? As we age, we typically experience unexpected changes in our bodies, hormones, and sexual desire that can shake up our sense of who we are and whether we are still virile, masculine, feminine, or womanly.

    For women, menopause can bring on a sense of loss as the childbearing stage of life draws to an end. And some women experience early menopause, or hormonal changes due to operations or medical treatments. Changes often serve as physical reminders that time is passing and our lives will not last forever. Consider whether this is an issue for you.

Bodies start to change as we reach midlife, and medical conditions can cause us to lose our fertility, libido, or sense of being good-looking or desirable. Sexuality is the foundation of bringing forth new life, so when sexuality wanes, or our sexual functioning is reduced, we can feel less attractive, powerful, and important. At this time in your life, you might want to imagine different ways you can be creative and bring forth something new.

Aging can be particularly difficult to accept when it affects our image of ourselves as powerful, attractive, and able to contribute to our community. Some people respond to these feelings of loss by trying to regain the bodies they once had. Some develop depression, which can be anger turned inward. Some are angry and express their anger outwardly in ways that make them feel powerful but perhaps guilty afterward. This chapter of our health story is often very closely tied to our stories about who we are and our place in the world.

Many physicians and health care providers do not address sexual concerns and body image with their patients, perhaps because it feels out of their area of expertise. They may be embarrassed or uncomfortable about bringing it up, or they may sense that their patients would be, if they were to open a dialogue. Consequently, many people suffer silently and unnecessarily.

For example, people with diseases and conditions who develop poor body image as a result of changes in their bodies would benefit from guidance on how to be more self-accepting. In menopause, eating disorders typically associated with adolescence and young adulthood—bulimia and anorexia, for example—are more common than many physicians might expect. Resistance to the process of aging and to changes in sexuality and hormones can contribute to a poor body image, which can be a trigger for these disorders.[5]

Without the distortions created by the ego getting in the way, an individual can better ascertain his or her body's true needs in terms of food and exercise.[6] One way to begin attaining freedom from unhealthy thoughts about weight and physical attractiveness in a culture that often overemphasizes these attributes is by doing work with chapter three of your health story.

71

CHAPTER 4: Symptoms Management for Various Health Conditions and Acute Ailments

You might have a chronic condition with symptoms, or simply occasional acute ailments not related to a condition. For example, some people have chronic pain and headaches associated with a disease they are living with and coping with. Others may not have a chronic condition but may occasionally get migraine headaches or a flare-up of pain in a shoulder injured long ago. You might have health ailments regularly due to medications you are on, your underlying condition, or both. You may occasionally experience a symptom and want to know more because you are seeing a pattern emerge. In all of these cases, answering the questions in this chapter of your health story can help.

- **What works/good habits.** When it comes to managing symptoms of a chronic condition, and avoiding acute ailments, what is working for you and what isn't? If you made some positive changes in the past that allowed you to better manage symptoms of a chronic condition, or that helped you avoid acute ailments, what were they? If you are experiencing an ailment right now, could it be related to a change in your habits?
- **Origin of challenges.** What is contributing to your challenges with managing symptoms and avoiding acute ailments? When did you first develop symptoms—or the ailment you are concerned about? What was going on in your life at the time?
- **Connections.** If you have a chronic condition, do you see any connection between your symptoms and another area of your health? For example, when you are giving into bad habits such as not getting enough exercise or rest, do your symptoms flare up? If you are experiencing an acute ailment, could it be indicating a health condition that you have recently developed, or that you had once, and thought you had overcome?
- **Being informed.** Do you know where to find helpful information about alleviating your symptoms or ailment? Are there steps you could take today to get better information and guidance?
- **Partnering.** Can you identify anyone who can partner with you in changing this chapter in the story of your health, such as a physician or specialist in your disease? Do you have support from people

around you in addressing your issues in this chapter of your health story? For example, are you in a support group for people living with your condition?

- **Dealing with changes that have occurred in your health condition.** What is the role of emotional stress in your chapter on symptoms management? How are your symptoms affecting your health, emotions, and beliefs about yourself? Which of your concerns about your symptoms have less to do with your physical health than with your discomfort with no longer being able to engage in activities you used to engage in and enjoy?

- **Genetics and family history.** How have your genetics or family legacy influenced your thinking about your symptoms or any acute ailments you are experiencing? For example, do you hold beliefs such as "Blood clots are common in my family, so I was probably destined to develop this problem," "We have weak constitutions in my family, so no wonder I have so many aches and pains," or "We don't live long in my family, so the symptoms I'm experiencing must be signs I am headed toward an early death"? Remember, you are not destined to live another's health story. Yours is unique.

- **Stress.** What is the role of stress in this chapter in your health story? How might you reduce your stress to improve this chapter?

- **Goals.** What, if any, goals do you have regarding managing your symptoms or addressing a particular ailment? Why did you choose those goals?

- **Payoffs to resisting change vs. payoffs to change.** If you are experiencing symptoms of a chronic condition and not managing them well, are there payoffs to that? If so, what are they? Can you imagine finding another way to achieve those payoffs?

    For example, if the people you love give you more attention when your symptoms flare up, could you find another way to get the attention you need? If you are experiencing an acute ailment, is there a payoff to having that ailment? For example, does having a headache or backache force you to slow down and relax, something you need to do but wouldn't if it were not for the ailment reminding you?

    If you have a chronic condition, are there payoffs to managing its symptoms that go beyond less pain and physical discomfort or better long-term health, such as having more independence, feeling more optimistic and positive about your life overall, and so on?

- **Identifying themes.** Can you identify some themes that are influencing this chapter in your health story? Are there themes associated with problems you are having with specific physical systems?

    For example, if you have lung and respiratory issues, figuratively speaking, are you feeling stifled and having trouble breathing? If you have skin issues, do things get "under your skin" or do you have an "itch" to do something? If you have vision issues, are you "not seeing clearly" or "being myopic"? If you have digestion issues, do you have trouble "stomaching" or "digesting" things? If you have chronic inflammation, could it be you are not fully acknowledging or not dealing with your "inflammatory" emotion, anger? If you are experiencing physical fatigue, are there stressors you are emotionally or mentally tired of dealing with that you need to release? Is your resentment or bitterness about things you can't resolve or fix tiring you out? If your immunity is low lately, could it be that your empathy is leading you to take in too many toxic or stressful emotions belonging to others, causing you to feel overwhelmed? Do you typically have worse symptoms at a particularly emotional or stressful time of the year, such as during the holidays or when an anniversary of a death or major loss comes around?

    In other words, look at your physical symptoms, condition, or physical systems and think about how any problems you have with them might be seen figuratively, as themes. You might also return to the earlier material on the chakras and consider whether there might be correspondences between certain physical symptoms and emotional issues and a particular area of the body, such as feeling there is a connection between your heartache and your cardiac health.

- **Your chapter's title.** Is there a saying, or song, book, or movie title, that summarizes what you are experiencing in regard to this aspect of your health? For example, would you say, "I'm winding down," "living on borrowed time," "It's always something—if it's not one thing, it's another," or "Anything that can go wrong with my body will—it's Murphy's Law"?

- **Concerns about mortality.** Does this chapter in your story of your health cause you to worry about your mortality? If so, why? Whatever the underlying reason for any physical deterioration, you may be able to slow and minimize it, and perhaps even reverse it, by making better health choices. Aches and pains, and the development of chronic health conditions or diseases, often serve as a physical reminder that time is passing and we will not live forever. Consider whether this is an issue for you. We will revisit the topic of aging in Chapter Eight: Revising the Story of Your Health.

Many diseases and acute and chronic conditions have thematic aspects, including the ones alluded to in these questions. For example, if you have diabetes or a prediabetic condition, you may need to work differently with archetypal energies associated with themes such as rebelliousness, which can make it hard to accept the dietary restrictions and need for more structure to your eating throughout the day. A theme of *puer aeturnus,* the perpetual child, might make you long for the freedom you had in the past to eat whatever foods you wanted, eat erratically throughout the day, and not have to plan snacks and meals in order to maintain stable mood, energy, and blood sugar levels.

People with breathing problems often experience anxiety because when symptoms are present, they are aware with each breath that they can't draw in the oxygen their body needs. You might also want to dialogue with your condition, your fear, your lungs, your breathing, or your inner healer to learn more and to alter the way archetypal energies are affecting you. (You'll find instructions on the practice of dialoguing in Chapter Four: Expanded-Awareness Practices for Gaining Insights and Energies.) You may need to work with such themes as courage, faith, and determination.

If you treat your symptoms and illnesses as adversaries, you will have a different relationship with them than if you think of them as potential allies that can help you learn, grow, or even heal in some way. Of course, an adversarial stance may be what you need when you are dealing with cancer or diabetes. But it can help to see cancer cells or viruses as just trying to survive, seeking nourishment. You might wish to dialogue with your symptoms or your condition to learn more about them and possibly negotiate a new relationship with them. You might also wish to work with the archetypal energy of endings to help your cancer cells or virus die. (See the journey to encounter the energy of endings in Chapter Eight: Revising the Story of Your Health.)

Other "Chapters" You Might Consider
Identifying and Exploring

Potentially, there are other chapters in your health story you might like to explore, such as genetic predispositions. You might also decide your health story has a chapter on anxiety and depression that is worth examining because those are affecting your immunity, sleep, and other aspects of your health. Let your intuition guide you in choosing any extra chapters to look at.

If you believe you have a genetic predisposition to a particular condition and wish to explore that chapter of your health story, you might answer the following questions:

- When it comes to taking care of yourself so you don't develop the health problem or condition you may have a genetic predisposition to, ask yourself, What have you done until now to prevent it from developing?

    What would you like to do? Would taking a test to determine whether you have a genetic predisposition to the condition motivate you to make changes in your health habits now? Would you be willing to take those actions to prevent the disease without being tested? If you took the test and it showed you did not have the gene or gene markers for a particular condition, would you take those actions anyway? If not, why not?
- If the story of your genetic predisposition had a title, what would it be? What would you like it to be? For example, is the title "Our family is cursed" while you would like it to be "I am going to change my family legacy"? Could you do healing work to minimize the possibility of expressing genes for the disease that runs in your family?

If you have anxiety and/or depression, or you experience these in relationship to a disease, condition, or illness and wish to explore that chapter of your health story, you might answer the following questions:

- Do you have occasional physical problems or health conditions you know or strongly suspect are related to anxiety or depression? If so, identify the problems or conditions.

- How are your physical problems or health condition related to anxiety or depression affecting other aspects of your health (weight, stamina, balance, strength, and so forth)? How are they related to your beliefs about yourself?
- Are there any payoffs to having anxiety or depression, or physical problems or a condition related to them? For example, does your anxiety cause you to focus on what you need to do to change the story of your health and even change the story of your life? Could you experience these benefits even if you didn't experience anxiety? Is there a payoff to being depressed, tired, and physically fatigued, such as avoiding the emotional discomfort of socializing or meeting new people or potential romantic partners?
- When it comes to managing your anxiety and depression, what has worked for you in the past? What is working for you now? Is there something you were doing in the past to manage it that you are not doing now? Why did you stop using that approach?
- What are the obstacles to managing your anxiety/depression and any physical challenges related to them?
- What are your goals for managing your anxiety/depression and any physical challenges related to them?
- If the story of your experience of your anxiety/depression and the physical challenges they are related to had a title, what would it be? What would you like it to be? For example, do you feel as if your story is "I'm so tired," but you would like it to be "It's getting better"?

Again, you might want to work on some of these questions now and come back to write more later, after having used some of the expanded-awareness practices in this book, as those are likely to provide you with valuable insights.

However you choose to work with this journaling chapter, whichever chapters of your health story you decide to explore, and whatever order in which you work with them, I hope you will dedicate the time needed to dig deep into multiple chapters in your health story. Doing so can help you learn more about the state of your health now and the origins of your health problems. Then, you will begin to have ideas about what you want to change in the future.

If you would like to write a new health story, it helps to know what you do and don't want to experience. You may have forgotten what it was like to be without health challenges, or without a specific health problem. Rather than assume you can't do anything about it and that you can't experience the level of health you had in the past, you can choose to write a new and better health story that does not incorporate the problem—migraine headaches, insomnia, excess weight, digestive issues, or whatever it is. That new health story can be brought to life, allowing you to have better health and a better relationship to your physical body. You can always add to or adjust your health story later, if you find out it is not working for you or if you realize it is too difficult to bring to life.

Now that you have identified your current health story, and perhaps some obstacles that have prevented you from changing it, the deeper work begins. In the next chapter, you will be introduced to expanded-awareness practices that can provide you access to transpersonal realms where you can discover insights and energy for writing a new, better health story. If transformation flowed easily, simply, and naturally from making a conscious decision to alter your lifestyle habits that affect your health, you probably would have changed them already. It is in the transpersonal realms where you gain the ability to understand and overcome the blocks that have been standing in your way.

Expanded-Awareness Practices for Gaining Insights and Energy

The way to access the invisible world, collective unconscious, or transpersonal realms is through expanded-awareness practices that alter consciousness. Altered states are often associated with feelings of profound well-being and rejuvenation, harmony within oneself or with nature, experiences of timelessness, and reduction of physical pain.[1]

Jungians and shamans would say that achieving these states has benefits beyond helping you to feel good: Altered states of consciousness can allow you to access insights and energies you can use to change your health story and achieve healing.

Traditionally, shamans or medicine men or women often worked with sacred plants such as Ayahuasca to assist people in accessing and doing work in transpersonal realms, because of these plants' ability to induce an altered state of consciousness. However, using these plants is not necessary for you to benefit from the expanded-awareness practices you will learn about here.

Music, both live and recorded, can assist you in shifting out of ordinary, everyday consciousness into a more trancelike state that will allow you to experience transpersonal realms and communicate with your unconscious and the collective unconscious. You might use drums and rattles, or recordings of drumming and rattling, to help you alter your consciousness when you use the expanded-awareness practices in this book—especially the journeys. Recorded nature sounds can be helpful for this purpose, too.

Also, consider using the expanded-awareness practices outdoors, in the presence of natural sounds, as these may be effective for shifting your consciousness and altering your brain waves. Wherever you choose to use a practice, be sure you will be uninterrupted for at least 20 minutes.

In these practices, you will find general directions that allow you to fill in the details. I have written them this way to give your unconscious the freedom to express itself. So, for example, if you are asked to ascend a mountain along a winding road, you might experience that as a sensation, a visual image (perhaps an animated one), or just an understanding or inner knowing.

You might wish to record some of the expanded-awareness practices, particularly the journeys with lengthy instructions, before using them. Speak the instructions into a recording device (such as a cell phone with a recording application), and make sure to leave pauses. When doing the journeys, you will want to have plenty of time for insights to appear after you take an action such as entering a chamber or asking a question.

You may want to be outdoors in nature when you use the practices, as that can enhance the experience. You will want to limit the possibility of disruptions, so turn off any devices or cell phone applications and make sure no one will disturb you. Finding solitude in nature is easier if you have access to private land that is removed from streets and other properties, but you can do these exercises in your own backyard or by a park near your home, or even indoors.

You might also wish to try journeying alongside others who are interested in doing it simultaneously. Be sure you agree on when and how the practice will end, so that you do not disturb each other as you have your separate experiences.

When using the practices, you might begin in a standing position but end up sitting or lying down. Don't feel you ought to sit in a certain position, or on the floor or ground. If you have joint discomfort or limited flexibility, simply sit comfortably, perhaps on a chair, cushion, or mat, if that helps you to focus on the practice rather than your physical discomfort.

I encourage you to prepare for the experience of an expanded-awareness practice by using these rituals, which you will learn about in this chapter:

- opening sacred space by invoking the four directions and the below and above
- cleansing your energy field
- doing mindful breathing

When you are finished using the practice, you will end by:

- closing sacred space

- thanking the energies that helped you (if that feels comfortable for you)
- not being too quick to analyze what happened

Again, I will explain all of the parts of these rituals. All combined, they can be done in just a minute or two—or you can take your time with them. As you begin to use an expanded-awareness practice, the rituals can be very effective in allowing you to shift your consciousness quickly. The closing ritual can help you to return to ordinary consciousness afterward and experience awe and gratitude for the power of the work.

In many wisdom traditions, you open sacred space when you intentionally designate the space around you as sacred, ritualistically delineating its boundaries. Shamans say opening sacred space creates a container for the energy you are working with, and closing it facilitates your return to ordinary reality. As you close sacred space, you might want to touch the earth or wait for a few moments to "ground" yourself before resuming your everyday activities. You do not have to use these rituals with every expanded-awareness practice in this book, or use them every time, but I will remind you here and there to consider them. I think they are especially helpful with the shamanic journeys.

PREPARATORY PRACTICE 1: How to Open (and Close) Sacred Space

Opening and closing sacred space, a practice drawn from shamanic traditions, is particularly helpful for a few reasons. First, it allows you to acknowledge your connection to the matrix (the energy field that connects all of creation and that originated from Source). Second, it can also help you to feel supported by the matrix and by Source. Third, intentionally invoking the energies of the various directions can assist you in feeling gratitude and a connection to Source.

In studying shamanism and being taught by various shamans, I have learned that indigenous cultures in the Americas each have their own unique ways of marking and working with sacred space. I work with the medicine wheel taught by the Healing the Light Body School, which is based on the one used by the Quechua people, who are the indigenous people of the Andes. The South represents shedding the stories of the past, regeneration, and healing old wounds. The West represents moving beyond the fear of death and the influences of the past, including the influences of past generations.

The North is associated with seeing our stories as journeys with meaning, and as being woven into larger stories we share with other people, including our ancestors. Observing these stories as journeys intertwined with other journeys is said to awaken us to our spiritual nature. The East corresponds with new possibilities for the future, beginnings, and new stories in which we have integrated all we have learned and experienced.

Practitioners begin in the South and make their way toward the East, finishing their invocation by acknowledging Mother Earth, or Pachamama, and Father Sky. When invoking Mother Earth, I thank her for all she does for me and ask to be guided in my stewardship. When invoking Father Sky and the great, ultimately unknowable Spirit of Life, I express my gratitude for being part of life's plan.

The four directions, and below and above, might be thought of as archetypal forces that can help you in your work. You can call them ritualistically with words such as:

To the South, I offer thanks and praise, and I call upon you to join me in my work as I let go of what no longer serves me.

To the West, I give you my gratitude and ask that you help me to overcome fear.

To the North, thank you, and thank you to the ancestors for handing down their wisdom. Help me to see my life as a journey. Help me to know you have given me a map.

To the East, thank you for the hope of new beginnings. Help me to see new possibilities and opportunities.

Praise and thanks to you, Mother Earth, and to you, Father Sky.

If you do not wish to use an invocation such as this one, you might simply allow images or words to flow naturally as you generate feelings of gratitude and hope while you face each direction in the order I have described. As you do this, invite in and be open to the energies associated with the South, West, North, and East and the below (Earth) and the above (Heaven).

You can also simply praise and thank God, your guardian angels, or the saints as you acknowledge, in order, each of the steps in a cycle of healing and renewal. The idea is to honor and invite in forces beyond yourself, as these can fuel transformation while you engage in a healing process that includes:

- letting go
- allowing fear to rise within you but not overwhelm you, as you release it
- observing that you feel a sense of interconnectedness and being part of a larger, shared story
- planting the seeds of something new and beginning to bring to life a new story (in this case, a health story)
- recognizing the power of your connection to the earth and what is available to you in the material world
- acknowledging the power of your connection to the sky and what is available to you in the realm of Spirit and consciousness

As you open sacred space, remain open to your perceptions of the qualities of the energies you are working with. In his book *Power Up Your Brain*, coauthored with neurologist David Perlmutter, shaman Alberto Villoldo suggests that in opening sacred space, you might simply face each direction and feel your connection to the energy each represents. He says, "Help your educated, logical brain understand that these are ancient personifications of the forces of nature."[2] In calling upon the energies of the six directions, or calling on Spirit, angels, or other emanations of Spirit, you can also set your intention to achieve insights and assistance regarding a particular health concern.

The traditional method of opening sacred space is to stand and pivot to invoke the four directions and the below and above, but you can also simply imagine yourself opening sacred space. However, acknowledging and honoring the four directions of the medicine wheel, as well as the below and above, as you walk in a circle or pivot in place, seeing from different angles, reminds you that everything is connected and there are many perspectives. I find it valuable to stand and face each of the four directions as I call them in or thank them for helping me in my work. I kneel when I acknowledge Mother Earth and raise my hands to the sky when I recognize the sky spirits and the Great Spirit.

To close sacred space, thank the energies that helped you, honoring them. If it's comfortable for you, do this by moving to face each direction as well as the earth below your feet and the sky above you. Closing sacred space will help you experience a sense of connection to all and also express gratitude for support.

If you decide to make recordings to guide you in using any particular expanded-awareness practice, you might want to include in the recording the words for opening (and later, closing) sacred space, as well as a reminder to use the next two steps in preparation: cleansing your energy field and breathing mindfully.

PREPARATORY PRACTICE 2: How to Cleanse Your Energy Field

Cleansing your energy field involves becoming more aware of your energy field and any disturbances in it you need to attend to. It can help free your mind from ordinary concerns and make it easier for you to explore what Jungians call the unconscious and what shamans might call transpersonal realms. A simple way to cleanse your energy field is to use the following technique, which employs the bright, white, healing light of Source.

To begin, reduce the intensity of your mind's activity. You might simply observe a simple scene within nature, or close your eyes and take a few deep breaths, focusing on the sensation of breathing as you inhale and exhale.

Next, do what is sometimes called a body scan: Observe with your intuition whether there are any areas in your energy body that seem heavy or dark, frayed or damaged, or that cause you to feel constricted, weighed down, heavy, sad, or upset. If so, retain your focus on that spot.

Inhale, imagining you are drawing in bright, white light that has a healing quality. As you exhale, send that dark, heavy energy outward. Repeat this until you feel any dark, heavy energy lifting or dissolving.

Then, focus on other areas where you might find this type of energy that you would like to release. When you pay attention to these spots, you may notice that they have an emotional quality to them—for example, they may have a quality of sadness or anxiousness. Continue cleansing your energy field until you feel it is free of any heavy or frayed spots.

PREPARATORY PRACTICE 3: How to Do Mindful Breathing

Most of us are unaware of how we breathe unless we consciously draw attention to it. However, if we practice mindful breathing, paying attention to the sense of inhalation and exhalation and the pause between the two, we can further shift our consciousness out of everyday awareness.

Mindful breathing does not require changing the pattern of your inhalations and exhalations. You can simply direct your attention to the experience of drawing in breath and naturally allowing yourself to exhale. Each time your awareness begins to wander, and you experience a thought—such as "I'm not sure I'm doing this right"—or a distraction, such as the sound of a dog barking in the distance—simply bring your awareness back to the sensation and experience of your breath.

You can also use mindful breathing techniques that involve counting as you inhale or exhale and controlling your breathing pattern. For example, you might breathe in for seven counts, hold your breath for seven counts, exhale for seven counts, and hold your breath again for seven counts. Another option for mindful breathing is to silently say one particular word as you inhale and exhale—"peace" or "balance," for example. However you do mindful breathing, the idea is to feel fully present in the moment as you consciously experience yourself inhaling and exhaling. As you do mindful breathing, you become aware that you are engaged in an exchange of energy between you and the world outside of you, of which you are a part. This awareness helps you shift out of everyday consciousness and experience an expansion of your awareness.

Again, after using an expanded-awareness practice such as shamanic journeying, close sacred space if you opened it and silently express gratitude for the experience. Then, after you feel you have returned to ordinary consciousness, give yourself some time to simply remember what happened when you were using the practice and, later on, write about the experience in your journal. You might also sketch any images that came to you and look at them, pondering their significance for you.

Taking a Journey to the Quiet to Balance Your Energy

In shamanic work for healing, balance is always a goal. We need to energetically remove something that causes poor health and place that energy somewhere—typically, we release it to the earth. We also have to energetically bring in something that promotes health in order to fill the space we just created. The healing energy we draw in is said to come from Source. Shamans say that the earth is able to transform unhealthy energies that we give it, so it is not harmed during our process of self-healing. And since

Source has infinite curative powers, we can draw upon it again and again to achieve balance.

Balancing energies is also intrinsic to Ayurvedic medicine and other traditional healing modalities. Even Western physicians recognize that for optimal health, we need balance—including in our diets and between our activity and rest.

The following practice for balancing energies involves taking something away and bringing something else in energetically. As you will recall from Maria's story, the Quiet is the place before creation, where all exists in potential before it has come into being in the material world. It is a comforting, healing place, where you will experience a sense of unconditional love for yourself and for all creatures—in fact, for all that exists in creation. The Quiet offers white, healing light that you can draw into your energy field.

Is the Quiet real? I believe so, and I often travel to it to take in the helpful energies it has in abundance. In fact, when I cleanse my light energy body, the white, healing light I draw in originates in the Quiet.

Before you start, clearly set an intention to travel to the Quiet to gain energies that can positively influence your physical health and discard any energies that are negatively influencing it. This energy exchange will bring your energy field back into a state of balance and wellness. Open sacred space, cleanse your energy field, and use a mindful breathing technique to shift your awareness.

EXPANDED-AWARENESS PRACTICE: JOURNEY TO THE QUIET

Visualize going through a long tunnel to a crystalline, diamond-like energy structure, and move through it into a place that you intuit to be the Quiet. There, experience the qualities of this transpersonal realm.
Ask the Quiet:

- "What message do you have for me about my health?"
- Wait for the answer to be revealed to you. Remain present and patient. Then, when you are ready, ask:
- "Is there anything more I need to know?"

Again, be patient and remain open.

Ask the Quiet to take away something you do not need and should let go of in order to experience better health.

Ask the Quiet to give you something you need that will help you experience better health.

When you feel you are finished, go back the way you came through the crystalline structure into the tunnel and back to where you started the journey. Thank the Quiet for helping you and then return to ordinary consciousness.

Close sacred space and take plenty of time to ponder what you experienced and learned. Journal about it and identify any insights into your health that you received.

Support for Your Use of Expanded-Awareness Practices

In many wisdom traditions, when you do a shamanic journey, you always have with you a supportive, protective guide. When you meet this spirit guide, you should ask it whether you have permission to continue. When looked at from a Western, psychological perspective, the idea of asking permission to explore the psyche makes sense if your conscious mind is not emotionally prepared to receive what awaits you. Spirit guides who require you to ask permission to have a journeying experience seem to serve as psychological protectors.

When you ask a guide permission to continue, usually, the guide will grant it, which means your unconscious feels you are ready to do this work and discover what is hidden from your conscious mind. If the guide you encounter does not grant permission, ask why, and inquire about what you might do to be allowed to continue. You can negotiate with the guide. If permission is still not given, you can try again another time—and journal about the reasons why your psyche might not want you to explore what is hidden from your conscious mind.

Often, when permission is not granted but you come back another day to take the journey, you meet no resistance. It might be that at this point, you are more emotionally prepared for what you will discover. In any case, there is no cause to feel trepidatious about encountering an inner figure who resists giving you permission to explore a transpersonal realm at a particular time.

For the journeys in this book, consider any guide you meet to be your inner healer, the wise aspect of yourself that knows what is necessary for you to achieve healing. Whatever form they take when you encounter them in transpersonal realms, guides are there to support you, so be grateful when they appear and thank them for their assistance.

Taking a Journey to the Lower World

Traditionally, a journey to the lower world, also known as a soul retrieval journey, might be undertaken to confer with energies of one's ancestors and animal spirit guides, connect with Earth energies, and retrieve lost soul parts, that is, aspects of yourself that split off and became lost due to past traumatic experiences. During a lower world journey, you can also access and release bound-up energy you want to positively influence the story of your health today and in the future. A Jungian might say you would also access aspects of yourself that became hidden from your conscious mind, lost in your shadow, because your conscious mind was deeply uncomfortable with them. Once retrieved, those qualities can then be reintegrated into your everyday awareness in a positive way.

Bringing forward what is hidden in the unconscious mind can be emotionally unsettling, and even sometimes frightening. Some of what is hidden may have been concealed from your conscious mind in order to protect you from having to face the pain associated with it—memories of abuse, for example, or knowledge about yourself that you find very uncomfortable. If you feel upset after using the practices here, you can always ask for help from Source. You can also consult a therapist to help you deal with the emotions that have arisen. Most of the time, however, journeying is an overall positive experience.

The lower world journey I will be describing features several chambers and a guardian spirit. In the chambers, you will encounter insights and energy that can take various forms, such as a symbol, an inner figure, a sensation, or an inner knowing. As you ready yourself for the journey, create an intention to learn about something from the past that is influencing your health today. Typically, you would discover the roots of your health story and something from your past that needs to be brought back into your everyday awareness. In each chamber, you can formulate the specific questions

I have suggested or simply have the intention to get the answers to questions about what from your past is influencing your health story today, what from your past you need to get rid of to experience a better health story, and what from your past you need to bring in.

Because this is an extensive and detailed journey, I want to remind you to consider recording it and playing back the recording when you want to actually take the journey. I encourage you, too, to prepare for it by opening sacred space, cleansing your energy field, and doing mindful breathing.

EXPANDED-AWARENESS PRACTICE: JOURNEY TO THE
LOWER WORLD

Envision a spiral staircase leading downward into the earth. See yourself descending this spiral staircase, going lower and lower, deep into the earth.

When you reach the bottom of the staircase, take a deep breath and look straight ahead. Before you is a guide: your inner healer. Observe this ally who will help you achieve the insights you seek and assist you in releasing energy you no longer need and bringing in energy you will find beneficial.

Ask your inner healer, "Do I have permission to continue my journey today?" If the answer is no, ask, "What do I need to do to gain permission?"

Wait for the answer, and decide whether you want to do what is asked of you. If you choose not to do what the guide asks, you can return up the spiral staircase to the world of ordinary consciousness and come back at another time.

If you receive permission, look in front of you and observe that there is a hallway you are entering, and that on your left, there are three doors in a row. With your inner healer, approach the first door and stand before it. Ask, "What factor or event from my past is influencing my current health and needs to be understood and dealt with?"

Pause. Then, open the door to reveal something that answers the question. It could be a symbol, a sensation, a word, or a figure. Remain there for a time, taking in the insights you are being given. You might wish to ask if there is anything else you need to know. You are in a place for receiving insights, so remain open to them.

> When you are ready, walk with your inner healer to the second door, and ask, "What do I need to get rid of from my past in order to achieve improved health?" Open the door to receive the answer. Take your time absorbing the insights.
>
> When you are ready, continue on to the third door, accompanied by your inner healer. As you stand in front of this final door, ask, "What do I need to bring in from my past, perhaps something that I once had and lost, so that I can achieve improved health?"
>
> Again, open the door to receive your answer. Be open to receive what you need, in whatever form it appears. Take your time absorbing the insights.
>
> Turn to your inner healer and thank it for being your guide and protector. Then, return to the spiral staircase and ascend it, climbing the stairs until you are back in your body, once again aware of your physicality. Thank Source for helping you on this journey.

If you opened sacred space, close it. Later, journal about what you experienced and what you learned about your health story—and how you might apply what you learned.

When I did this lower world journey, in the first chamber, I was immediately struck by how my health was influenced by my parents' smoking. I also had a sense that my mother drank alcohol while she was pregnant with me. I think that at the physical and metaphorical levels, those factors gave me a sense of constriction. They may have played out in vascular disease for me, with plaque buildup that restricts blood flow. Psychologically, I have sometimes experienced a sense of constriction and felt a strong desire to live more expansively.

Another environmental factor I became conscious of involved growing up in Pittsburgh when there was much air pollution. In the midafternoon during the 1940s and 1950s, the sky would be dark from smog from the mills, and sooty grease would accumulate on car windows. I had high levels of lead in my blood, and sometimes I had a sense of mental fogginess. I compensated by exerting my intellect, but I had to use extra effort to overcome these factors, affecting my ability to think clearly and without constriction. I also suspect that my immune system was weakened by my parents' health habits and the pollution I experienced growing up because I had more than my share of childhood illnesses.

In the second chamber, the immediate message was that I need to get rid of clutter. I tend to hold onto ideas, journals, books, and information from the past that I always intended to do something with, but seldom have I followed through on that intention. I need to take time to organize some of it and purge the rest of it because, metaphorically, the clutter adds to my constriction. In turn, the clutter can build up and impede my flow of energy. Sludge can build up energetically for anyone who holds onto clutter from the past.

The third chamber contains what you need to bring back from the past. In this chamber, I discovered that I need to bring back the light I used to experience before I took on the burden of many responsibilities. The light was like a lightness of being or sense of freedom. I realized I have to let light in energetically and clear out the clutter that is impeding it, so that I have space for the light to come in. I need to imagine myself being in light and actually get out into the sunlight in nature more often.

When I got back from my lower world journey and was further meditating on what I should be doing as a result of the information I received, I realized I need to drink more fluids, so I began to drink more water.

Another thing I've been called to do as a result of insights I received through journeying and meditating is to move my body. I now dance to my recordings of '50s and '60s songs, and as I dance, I combine my martial arts and qigong practices into a spontaneous series of movements. At the literal and psychological level, as I move, I am playing with the metaphors of constriction, rigidity, and imbalance to move toward expansiveness, flexibility, and balance.

If you encounter something while on a shamanic journey that you would like to learn more from, you can ask it more questions than the ones provided. I prefer to keep the number of questions to a minimum during the experience itself and then, later, dialogue to receive further insights from what I encountered.

How to Dialogue

Dialoguing is a key expanded-awareness practice, based on the technique of Jungian active imagination. Jungians would say dialoguing allows your conscious mind to access wisdom in your unconscious and to learn from it.

You might engage in dialogue with:

- an inner figure, power animal, or symbol you encountered during a journey, as long as the inner figure is not an actual person living or dead (more on that shortly)
- an emotion or emotional experience (for example, resistance, denial, or acceptance)
- a habit
- your disease or symptoms of your disease or a medical condition
- an acute ailment
- your inner healer (your innate ability to heal and repair your body and psyche)

The actual dialogue begins when you ask a question of a symbol, sensation, inner figure, emotion, habit, or inner healer you wish to dialogue with. What you intend to dialogue with answers you with wisdom that is hidden from your conscious mind and accessed through your unconscious. You continue asking questions, waiting for answers, and letting the conversation between your ego self (which uses its rational abilities to formulate questions) and your unconscious (which answers the questions) flow easily and naturally. Let follow-up questions naturally suggest themselves. When you feel ready to end the conversation, thank whatever you were dialoguing with, as this demonstrates respect for the process.

During your dialogue, you might ask, "What do I need to let go of energetically to improve my health?" and "What do I need to bring in energetically to (improve my health, live according to a better health story, get back on track with my vow to change my eating habits, and so forth)?" You might also ask, "What can I do for you?" and "What can you do for me?" The answers may help you better understand what you need to let go of or bring in or they may yield very different responses, such as "You can honor me by letting go of your shame about your body's appearance and its frailties right now" or "What you can do for me is stop denying my existence! I'm here to remind you to get more rest, and I will show up again to nudge you to take care of yourself." You never know exactly how a dialogue will unfold and what your unconscious will say to you.

In addition to your ego consciousness and whatever is speaking to you from your unconscious (such as a symbol or emotion), there is a third participant in the dialogue: your witnessing self. As the dialogue unfolds, this aspect of your awareness notices all that is happening. It may recognize your resistance to the process or your discomfort with what you are learning, and in turn, alert your ego consciousness, which can then choose to ask questions to learn more about those responses.

If you become uncomfortable because the dialogue is challenging for your ego consciousness, you can continue or end the dialogue. You can come back later and resume it if you wish. Keep in mind, however, that simply observing your resistance or discomfort may be enough to allow you to manage those challenges as the dialogue continues.

If you don't like the answer to a particular question, you can negotiate with whatever you are dialoguing with. For example, you might say to your inner healer, "But I don't want to do what you are asking of me. Isn't there something else I can do instead?" If you don't understand an answer, ask for clarification or more information.

Be patient with this process, and remain open to the timing of the answers and how they come to you. If you have trouble getting answers to your questions, it may be because you need to employ the techniques I have suggested for achieving a state of expanded awareness: opening sacred space, cleansing your energy field, and doing mindful breathing, perhaps while listening to music that helps you make the shift into an expanded-awareness state. If you are already using these techniques, consider whether you are rushing the process and not taking enough time to shift your consciousness.

You can simply have the dialogue in your head, as I have just described. However, you can also use a stone, two chairs, and physical movement to assist you in the dialogue as you work within sacred space.[3] The stone would serve as a physical representation of the inner figure or symbol you want to dialogue with, embodying its wisdom and energy. Sometimes, people find it easier to dialogue when working with the stone and using the chairs to change their perspective and position during the process.

To use these props to facilitate the dialogue, place two chairs opposite each other and choose a stone into which you will blow the energy of that which you want it to represent—for example, your inner healer, a symbol or figure, or your symptoms or ailment.

When you have readied yourself by focusing your intention on having a dialogue, hold the stone and blow into the stone the energy with which you wish to dialogue. Then, place the stone on the chair opposite you.

Sit in the first chair, facing the stone on the chair opposite you, and ask a question of what is now embodied by the stone—for example, your inner healer or the symbol, figure, symptom, or ailment you feel you can learn from. Ask, "What message do you have for me?"

Stand and walk over to the opposite chair, imagining that your ego awareness is being left behind in the other chair and that when you pick up the stone and take a seat in the second chair, you will embody the wisdom of the symbol, figure, emotion, and so forth contained within it. Pick up the stone, and sit down in the chair facing the one you were just in. Embody the energy and wisdom contained in the stone you are holding in your hands.

Let your unconscious mind awaken, and let the answer to the question your ego consciousness just asked come to you. Discover what your fear can tell you, what your inner healer can reveal, or what your insomnia or fatigue have to say.

Once you have intuited the answer to your question, say it out loud. Then get up, place the stone back on the chair, and return to the other chair, where you will let your ego consciousness come up with another question. Again, leave your chair to pick up the stone and access the energy it now embodies as you sit in the second chair. Wait for the answer to reveal itself to you, and ask for clarification or more information if you feel you need it.

Continue this process, using the questions suggested earlier and allowing the dialogue to flow naturally. Let your intuition guide you as to the best questions to ask, and how many to ask. Each time you ask a question, wait for an answer before returning to your position as the questioner.

With dialoguing, or any expanded-awareness exercise in which you ask questions, remember to be open to the answers appearing in a variety of ways, including as symbols, inner figures, and words that may confuse you at first. An inner healer might appear to you as yourself—perhaps looking wise or authoritative—or as a physician, a mother figure, or even an object. One man variously saw his inner healer as a younger, more vibrant and optimistic version of himself, as a scrawny black bird, or as his mother. In further dialogues with these images, he realized that all of them were manifestations of a "single deep core energy of peace and love." In a dialogue, or afterward, you may come to understand your inner healer's unusual or unexpected appearance. Moreover, you can dialogue with the figure or symbol more than once, and ask it directly why it appears as it does, or why its appearance changed in subsequent dialogues.

By patiently keeping your awareness in the moment as you encounter an inner healer or symbol or figure, or whatever you are dialoguing with, you set the stage for insights to appear. If you find emotions rising in you as you ask questions and receive answers, express those emotions. What you are dialoguing with is most likely to continue providing answers, even if you are angry, hurt, or afraid; in fact, it will probably convey soothing and reassuring messages.

Although you can dialogue with just about any type of inner figure, if it represents a real person—someone you know, perhaps, or a famous person—do not dialogue with it. You might somehow connect with that person's energy and influence this individual without getting permission to do so. Instead, dialogue with your feelings about that person to discover why that figure appeared to you.

Some people might ask whether the answers to your questions are coming from you, and if so, does that mean they are not guided by a greater wisdom and should not be trusted? It is up to you to decide whether these experiences are real, and where the answers emanate from—perhaps from God, or your inner healer that is always connected to Source. You might decide that whatever the source of this wisdom, you can trust it. It is not for me to tell you what to believe or how to interpret your experiences. But I have seen this process be invaluable to many people, so I encourage you to be open to the possibility that you are, in fact, accessing wisdom from an aspect of yourself known as the inner healer.

What You Might Learn from Dialoguing

By having a complete dialogue with several questions beyond just "What should I let go of, and what should I bring in?" you can delve deeper into what your health story is and how you can change it.

Anne, a woman I worked with, was experiencing hearing loss and feared her condition would worsen. She decided to dialogue with her fear of losing her hearing. Through this dialogue, Anne discovered what she was most afraid of was being disconnected from people. She dialogued further and learned the origin of that fear lay in her past: Her mother had lost her hearing, and Anne regretted not making more of an effort to interact with her mother after that happened. Anne equated her hearing loss to being isolated in a lonely, dark space—"almost like being in the birth canal," she explained. She realized her fear was a child's fear of being disconnected from her mother. At the end of the dialogue, Anne recognized she had gained images to work with further and had much more to explore. She became less afraid of losing her hearing because she realized that even if she could not avoid experiencing it, she could avoid being lonely or isolated.

A man named Harris decided to dialogue with his diabetes. The dialogue went something like this:

HARRIS: I know I should stick to my diet, exercise regularly, and reduce my stress. I always mean to do it, but somehow, I fail to do so. What can you tell me about that?

DIABETES: You know what you need to do.

HARRIS: Yes, but why don't I do it?

(The diabetes did not answer him, which can happen.)

HARRIS: Can you help me stick to my goals, so I can develop new habits and sustain them?

DIABETES: Yes. But it is up to you to make the choices that keep me under control.

HARRIS: How do I make better choices?

DIABETES: Stop fighting me. Acknowledge me.

HARRIS: I don't like having you, diabetes. I fight you—you're right. I hate having to restrict my diet and plan my meals and check my blood sugar. But you are not going away. I know that.

DIABETES: No, I am not.

HARRIS: But can I do something for you, to have a better relationship with you?

DIABETES: Acknowledge me.

HARRIS: Okay. I hear you. Can you help me better manage you?

DIABETES: Yes, if you are willing to acknowledge and accept me. I can help you by alerting you to when you are not taking care of yourself and your body's needs. I can signal you to let you know you are not managing your stress.

HARRIS: I never thought of that. Do you have any other messages for me?

DIABETES: Listen to me. Respond to me. Have a good relationship with me, so you can live well.

HARRIS: Thank you for giving me these insights.

DIABETES: You can always dialogue with me to learn more. I hope we talk again.

As a result of this dialogue, Harris began to accept and acknowledge his condition instead of denying it. It became easier for him to catch himself whenever he was breaking his vow to watch his diet, exercise more, and improve his stress management. His relationship with his diabetes became less adversarial and more collaborative.

A woman named Leslie decided to dialogue with her pain from fibromyalgia to learn more about it and perhaps establish a new relationship with it.

LESLIE: What message do you have for me?

PAIN: I am with you for now. You have much to learn from me.

LESLIE: I don't want to continue feeling pain. What do I have to let go of so that I can stop feeling pain?

PAIN: Anger. You are rigid, not fluid, because of your anger. And impatience. You are stuck in judgment and anger.

LESLIE: Can you tell me more about being fluid instead of angry? I'm not sure I understand.

PAIN: You are looking to blame someone because you are resisting what happened—your fibromyalgia that brought me to you. You are impatient with yourself and others. Your need to judge brought me to you. I am with you so that you can learn to stop judging and being angry. You get stuck there!

LESLIE: Who am I judging?

PAIN: People who place demands on you. Your healers who are not curing you of your disease. Yourself. You are very hard on yourself and have always been so. You feel you have to prove your worth now, even as you felt you had to prove your worth as a child, so you are harsh with yourself whenever you are in pain and distracted or weak.

LESLIE: It's hard to hear this. But you're right. I can't seem to accept myself. What can I bring in to change that?

PAIN: Patience and self-love. You need to learn your value outside of your ability to be productive. You are valuable when you are sitting and resting, doing nothing for others.

LESLIE: I will try to remember that. But I'm scared because I feel like you will be with me forever. I don't like how you limit me.

PAIN: You limit yourself when you judge yourself. Let go of your self-judgments, and you will see that some of your limitations disappear.

LESLIE: What can you give me to help me let go of my need to judge myself and other people harshly?

PAIN: I can give you the gift of awareness. When you feel pain, stop and remember how impatient and judgmental you are. In that moment, let go of judgment. Choose to be patient, fluid, accepting—accepting of yourself, of the moment.

LESLIE: What can I do for you?

PAIN: Let go of your need to judge. Do not judge yourself. Simply choose to let the judgment go when it arises in you. Then I won't have to show up and remind you to be patient and less judgmental. You will know when it is time to rest, and you will encounter me less often.

LESLIE: Thank you for helping me. I feel less angry. I feel better about myself. I don't feel you right now.

PAIN: I am not here to hurt you but to help you. I will stay with you only as long as you need me to.

LESLIE: I would like that. Thank you for helping me. I'm less afraid now and can accept that you will be with me to some degree. I can use you as a tool to check in with myself.

PAIN: I can remind you that you deserve to stop and focus on yourself and not just always focus on other people's needs.

LESLIE: Thank you. I needed that reminder. I am going to remember that whenever I encounter you in my daily life!

In any dialogue, themes are likely to arise, and those can be explored later to achieve more insights and work with the energy differently in order to improve your health story. If a woman were to have a dialogue similar to the one you just read, she might decide she needs to learn more about patience and how to develop it. A trip to the lower world could help her discover the origins of her impatience, let go of an obstacle to becoming more patient, and bring in the energy of patience. In turn, this might help her make better decisions about whether to continue working with a particular healer or using a particular treatment, rather than letting her impatience cause her to jump from doctor to doctor and medication to medication. It might also help her to be more patient with herself and her imperfections, allowing her to let go of stress that can exacerbate the pain response.

Don't be disappointed by what does or doesn't appear or what messages you receive when you are dialoguing. When you use this practice, you will often get in touch with painful feelings and truths about yourself. You won't always get the answers you would like—just as you will not necessarily experience what you expect or desire when you take a shamanic journey. Yet the insights you gain from dialoguing, challenging or disappointing though they may be, can help you make changes you may not have realized you need to make.

Let's say that on a journey to discover insights and energies affecting the story of your health, you come across a black cat. It could be a symbol of bad luck, which is its traditional association in the West. It would be easy to simply interpret it that way. But in a dialogue with it, you might realize its message for you is not "Accept that you simply experienced bad luck, and that's why you became sick." The dialogue might go something like this:

YOU: What can you tell me about the pain in my back that first showed up when I slipped and fell on the ice when walking?

BLACK CAT: The accident was no accident. The pain will not go away until you stop looking for something or someone other than yourself to blame.

YOU: What was my role in the accident?

BLACK CAT: You were not listening to your instincts when you went walking on that icy sidewalk. You wanted to prove you were independent, so you didn't want to ask for a ride home from your friend. You don't like to depend on others, and you don't want to admit your balance isn't what it used to be. You chose to deny that.

YOU: I can accept what you are saying. My pride got in the way. But I want my back to stop hurting. What do you want from me?

BLACK CAT: I want you to depend on others, instead of letting your pride get in the way. Asking others for help allows them to do something for you and feel proud that they have something to offer.

YOU: Do I need to let go of something?

BLACK CAT: Your fear. You make your own bad luck when you hold on to fear.

YOU: Will you give me something that can help me heal my back?

BLACK CAT: I will give you reassurance that you are not becoming old and dependent on others for your health and safety. You make yourself old when you refuse to dance. You sit, and your balance deteriorates. I want you to dance, play, and move your body freely again.

YOU: What can I do for you?

BLACK CAT: Give me permission to jump and play again. I'm not afraid of looking foolish. Let me dance around, leap, and run. Dance with me.

YOU: What do I need to bring in?

BLACK CAT: Playfulness!

YOU: Thank you for helping me, Black Cat. I will let you dance, and I'll dance and play with you.

An accident may seem to have happened completely outside of your control but actually be the result of neglecting yourself in some way. Many diseases and ailments don't appear suddenly; instead, they have been developing for some time before symptoms appeared. The conscious mind resists the idea that we had a role in our "bad luck" or in developing our illness or condition. By interacting with archetypal energies, you can learn about any energetic origins of your health challenges and the patterns or behaviors you need to change.

You might also discover that while you simply experienced "bad luck," the development of the condition offers the opportunity to change patterns you ought to have changed because they were not serving you. You do not have to experience what some call "New Age guilt"—guilt stemming from the idea that every problem you face was one you attracted or made manifest through your beliefs and actions.

Whatever you might have brought into being through unconscious beliefs and the influences of archetypal energies that you were not aware of is not something to feel guilty about. When you recognize you may have unconsciously played a role, however small, in manifesting an illness, be forgiving of yourself. Then, choose to work with archetypal energies to negotiate a better relationship with them. Perhaps you will be able to reverse the illness or arrest it before it turns into something more serious.

Dialoguing with an Emotion

Often, concerns about health involve fear. We tend to deny our fears, yet in dialoguing with them, we may gain insights that reduce our fear's power over us.

A man named Nick had extreme anxiety about his health and the possibility of developing cancer. This anxiety had been with him since childhood and was amplified by post-traumatic stress disorder (PTSD), which he had suffered from for years. Through dialoguing with his fears, he came to see his fear as a distinct energy that was separate from him. This allowed him to see he could make choices about whether or not to let the fear overcome him. The energy of his fear taught him that he doesn't have to constantly battle fear but can check in with it from time to time to remind himself to follow good health habits. When he realized he could change his relationship with fear to a friendlier one, he came to see how his struggles with his fear made him a more whole person who could be more compassionate toward other people's suffering.

A woman named Karen dialogued with her fear of getting older and becoming frail, and came to realize that she needed to stop denying this fear, or distracting herself from it, and instead, gently acknowledge it. She gained insights into how she can better take care of herself, such as telling her business partners and clients that she had to take time off and get knee surgery. Karen had been postponing it out of fear that she would be seen as unreliable and weak. Because of her dialogue, she came to recognize that her fears about people judging her were fears about being seen as not valuable in the way a younger woman in perfect health was. Karen realized that fear was irrational, because she was contributing to her business by providing wisdom born of experience.

A man named Jack dialogued with his fear of dying alone, without friends or family. He learned he needed to make space for himself and his own needs, including the need to engage in hobbies he loved. He also learned he needed to spend less time helping others at the expense of his own needs and desires, and he needed to stop participating in mindless activities to mask his fears. Consequently, he began to give more priority to the activities he loved, and he stopped automatically saying "yes" whenever someone asked him to do something for them. Although he could not completely overcome his fears, or ensure that he would never become old and lonely, he was able to live a better health story with less stress. He stopped overcommitting himself and began saying "no" more often so he could engage in self-care, which made him feel relaxed, revitalized, and happy.

Using the Arts to Engage Symptoms, Conditions, Ailments, or Inner Figures

In her book *Addiction to Perfection,* Jungian analyst Marion Woodman talks about accessing the unconscious through dancing. She writes, "Body movements ... can be understood as a waking dream. In its spontaneous movements the body is like an infant crying to be heard, understood, responded to, much as a dream is sending out signals from the unconscious."[4]

You could also use singing, painting, or another art to connect with these messages. Whether or not you are good at sketching, dancing, or writing poetry, you can engage and gain insights from archetypal energies through the use of the arts. Creative expression can help you discover more about your symptoms and ailments or your feelings. You might write a sonnet or free-form poem to your inner healer or make a sculpture or painting that represents your relationship to your cancer. You could write a song about the wheelchair you are using or about the loss of your hair due to chemotherapy.

When you allow your unconscious to speak through the arts, pay attention to any symbols that you sense are significant for you. If you think that the trees you find yourself sketching again and again may be telling you something about your challenges with fatigue, explore that. Similarly, if you start dreaming of trees, you might make drawings or paintings of them, or sculpt trees, and see if any insights emerge.

You might want to set an intention to work on a general or specific health problem by dancing with the energy of your health challenge. Another option is to dance in such a way as to achieve relief from your arthritis or to gain more stamina or a greater sense of well-being. Put on some music, and allow yourself to move with it naturally and intuitively. Trust that your body, inner healer, and Source will provide you with the experience you need to take away what you do not want and bring in what you desire. Let the wisdom of your body express itself.

Afterward, use your mind to understand what happened. Dialogue with the experience or with an image or sensation that occurred to learn more.

You can also dialogue with how your body moves in the dance. What might your undulating arms, swaying pelvis, or nodding head tell you about your health and your relationship to your physical body?

Similarly, you might want to work with singing as a way of engaging your symptoms' energies. You do not necessarily have to compose a song, but you could observe whatever notes or syllables emerge naturally from you after you set an intention to sing for your health.

You might include in that intention to have your song, or your spontaneous singing, help you let go of something and bring in something. You might discover you are letting go of fear as you sing a note, and bringing into yourself a positive energy that is shifting your mood and perspective, making you feel grateful for being alive and well. Sing whatever sounds you need to express. Is your inner healer expressing itself through your vocalization? If so, what is the message? What sound does your back pain or cancer make as you sing its song? Use dialoguing to work with your experience—its images and sensations, and any emotions wrapped up with it—to understand their meaning to you and your health.

One woman, Denise, found that a particular belly dancing move, using her pelvis to make an infinity sign, helped her get in touch with her feeling that her life was a part of a larger human experience of women teaching and supporting other women. The joy she felt in reconnecting with this sense of being part of something larger than herself helped her stay committed to her choice to get exercise during the winter months by doing belly dancing indoors. For her, dialoguing was unnecessary, because she gained an insight that was enough to make her begin thinking about ways to do belly dancing more often.

I've studied qigong and the martial arts for many years and learned many movement routines. Now when I practice these movement arts, I often let myself be led to move in whatever way seems right at the time. Sometimes I do the moves to music. I get aerobic, strength, balance, and flexibility benefits from doing this. Playful, spontaneous body movement can be healing in and of itself. Sometimes I just chant or sing whatever I feel called to. I let myself be "sung" just as I let myself be "danced."

If you have a disease or a health condition, you might want to dance to express your illness through movement and then dance as if you are healed. How do your dances differ? What can you do to ensure that how you move through your daily life more closely resembles the second dance?

What if you were to choose a theme from your health story to work with via the arts? You might set the intention to free yourself of constriction and being unable to breathe freely, and write poems about freedom and breath—or dance to learn about liberating yourself from the restrictions of a lung condition that is affecting you.

Using the arts, you could also learn more about your current health story and the one you might want to live according to. You might take crayons, paints, or markers and a piece of paper and create a work of art to express your health story, and what you would like it to be. Alternatively, use photographs and glue to do this. If you end up making a drawing, painting, or collage about what you would like to experience in your health story, consider keeping your visual creation in a spot where you can look at it regularly and remind yourself of the new health story you would like to bring to life. Notice what it feels like to sit or stand before it, drinking in its images and words. Do you feel hopeful? Resistant?

Why not write poetry about what you are experiencing or what you would like to experience in your health story? The poem could be free form, or it could rhyme, or you could even sing it. It might be a haiku. Traditionally, haiku—a Japanese poetry form—consists of five syllables in the first line, seven in the next, and five in the last, and is about nature. You might find that when you write poems about nature, you are writing about yourself and some aspect of wellness or imbalance.

You gain some distance from your health issues by working with them "outside" of you in the form of art, music, and movement. Each act of engagement may allow you to better understand the meaning of your symptoms or any health challenges, to help change them, and to learn to coexist with them. Perhaps your illness will not be cured, but you have consciously incorporated it into your life in such a way that you are no longer fragmented by it, are more at peace, and are freer to enjoy other aspects of your life.

Archetypal Energies and Spirit Animals

Indigenous people have often identified certain animals as having particular traits, associating the fox with the trickster and cleverness, for example, or associating the bison with strength and steadiness. These animal figures have been referred to as power animals or spirit animals, terms I use interchangeably. As with any symbol or figure, keep in mind that what any particular animal means to you could be different from what it means to another person.

In my last book, *Change Your Story, Change Your Life,* I told the story of a woman, Jean, who set an intention to journey and meet a spirit or power animal that would represent the qualities of an animal she needed to embody, and which, if better understood, could help her to achieve power in her own life. She was disappointed to meet a mouse because she associated it with being timid, inconsequential, and commonplace—hardly powerful! Jean remained open to the possibility that the mouse's attributes, or archetypal energy, served her in some way.

By dialoguing with this spirit animal, she came to understand that for her, it represented her humility, perseverance, and ability to work hard when facing a challenge. These were aspects of herself she had overlooked and that served as strengths. She came to better understand that to be more powerful in her life, she did not have to be a bear or lion. She could be who she was, and make good use of her humility, perseverance, and ability to work hard in times of challenge.

You might set an intention to encounter and work with a spirit animal, via a journey or when you are out in nature. Doing so can help you discover how you can write and bring into being a better story of your health.

My friend Marv Harwood, a shaman who was trained by a Blackfoot elder and medicine man, has told me he has his clients work with an animal in conjunction with a physical or psychological problem they might have. To do this, they choose an animal, letting their instinct or intuition guide them as to which animal to use. He then encourages the client to spend time watching, studying, and emulating that animal. They let those observations made at the intuitive level give them guidance as to what they should be doing for their personal healing.

For example, if someone were to choose a deer to help him, he might look at how the deer hesitates before taking action and then moves swiftly. Perhaps one of the issues for someone is that he rushes into things without pause and this habit is somehow affecting his health. Marv has seen in his healing practice that lessons like this have been profoundly life-changing for his clients.

If you would like to work with an inner figure of an animal, you could use the following exercise, based on one Marv Harwood shared with me. You might try it at home—or in a natural setting outdoors, where an actual animal might appear to you in response to your setting the intention to find an animal whose energy can help you address a health issue.

To prepare for this practice, I suggest you open sacred space, cleanse your energy field, and do mindful breathing to awaken your ability to access your unconscious mind.

EXPANDED-AWARENESS PRACTICE: ENCOUNTERING AND WORKING WITH A SPIRIT ANIMAL

Visualize that you are walking through a quiet, dark forest toward a clearing up ahead into which sunlight is streaming. As you come nearer, you hear the sounds of a waterfall. Step out of the forest into the clearing, and look around you at this beautiful, natural space, drinking it in. A waterfall is coming down a rocky hillside and spilling into a large pool.

Next to it, there is a boulder you can climb onto and sit upon. Walk toward it and take a seat there, feeling the sun-warmed stone beneath you and the cool mist of the waterfall on your face.

Ask this place, "Will you bring me an animal that can help me to heal?"

Remain on the rock, and look around you until you see an animal appear. It may be large or small. Notice how it moves as it approaches you and stops. It is waiting for you.

Simply observe it as it begins to move again. What is it doing?

Remain present with it. You might want to ask it what message it has for you, what you can do for it, and what it can do for you—and what you should release energetically and what you might bring in. Let your intuition guide you in deciding which questions to ask it, if any, or whether to simply be present with it, observing.

Walk toward the forest accompanied by the energy of the animal, not the animal itself. Continue walking, through the forest, until you are back in ordinary reality. Absorb this spirit animal's energy into your energy field, and thank it for helping you.

Close sacred space and contemplate what you experienced. Later, you can write in your journal about the encounter. You might reflect on what qualities the animal displayed, and what those qualities mean for you. Answer these questions in your journal: How did the animal move? Do you need to move that way? What qualities did it allow you to take into your energy field? How can these qualities help you in changing your health story?

You can also dialogue with the animal during the journey or afterward. If you do this, remember to ask it not only what message it has for you but also what you need to release, or give to it, and what you need to bring in, that is, what it can give you. As always, allow the dialogue and your wording of the questions to flow naturally.

To work with animals to gain insights and energies for healing, you might choose to energetically engage with an animal living with you or that you encounter when you are outside in nature. Use your intuition to tune into their consciousness. Ask the animal, "What message do you have for me about my health?" and listen for the answer. Ask, "What do you need me to let go of?" and then, "What do you need me to bring in?" Be open to the answers, which may not be what you might expect. For example, a squirrel is industrious and gathers and stores nuts for the winter. However, in dialoguing with or working with an actual squirrel or a squirrel as a spirit animal, you might find its message to you is not to be more productive but to let go of your anxious habit of scurrying away when you feel you are being watched or judged, and to bring in confidence as you go about your business, trusting that you will get done the work that needs to get done. In the context of health and your health story, this message could be about making changes to how you express your sexuality and confidence in your body without worrying about what others think of you and how you are changing.

How to Use Dreams to Achieve Insights for Your Health Story

Jungians and shamans work with dreams, as do practitioners of many wisdom traditions, to achieve insights. You can use dreams to gain information helpful for writing a new story of your health.

There are many cases of people having dreams that alerted them to health conditions, whether it was cancer or something else. If you have a dream that you suspect might be a warning that a physical ailment has developed, I strongly encourage you to check it out with a physician. Even so, keep in mind that the dream may not be literal. If a woman dreams of her right breast having a painful spot, it could be a warning sign of cancer or a precancerous condition that has developed in that breast. However, it could also be that her unconscious is telling her that her heart is hurting, figuratively speaking. It could be telling her that she has unresolved hurt or pain that is related to a theme of nurturing. (Her breast might, for her, symbolize nurturance and giving to others.)

Often metaphorical and physical meanings are related, and dialoguing with a specific pain can perhaps yield insights that will prove helpful, regardless of what medical tests show. In the case of the woman with the breast pain, even if there were no underlying physical condition, looking at her habit of giving too much to those who do not reciprocate would probably have value for her. If she does have an underlying condition, the emotional healing that would come from breaking the old habit might, perhaps, slow the development of the condition or perhaps reverse it. If you sense your dream has a message for you, honor the experience. Pay attention to the dream, and consider dialoguing with a symbol in your dream to learn more.[5]

You can also set an intention to have a dream that gives you insight into your health. Do this before you fall asleep, and if you wake up and remember a dream, record it right away, by writing it down or using a recording device. Focus on recording as many details, sensations, and emotions as you can recall.

When you can no longer remember anything else from or about the dream, it is time to ponder the meanings of the symbols, your emotions, and the plot. I suggest you avoid using a dream dictionary or analyzing the experience prematurely, for the conscious mind will often impose upon a dream its limited ideas about what the dream means. You might have a unique experience of a symbol that contradicts the usual interpretation. For example, a dream dictionary might tell you that to dream of a magnifying glass means you should look closely at details of a situation. However, for you, it might mean you should have your eyes checked.

Let's say you dreamed of a pipe in your brain being clogged or ready to burst. It could be a harbinger of a stroke or aneurism, so I strongly suggest you discuss this kind of a dream with a doctor and consider getting medical testing. Yet, at the metaphorical level, the clogged pipe could symbolize a blockage in your mind-body connection, or a problem with the energy or information you are feeding your brain, or something else. Through dialoguing with the clogged pipe, you could learn more and begin to address the issues it represents. After doing the work and checking out whether you have any health problems concerning your brain and its blood flow, you might set a conscious intention to have a dream in which your unconscious mind gives you information about the previous dream regarding the clogged pipe and any emotional issues you felt it symbolized. Perhaps you will dream that the pipe has cleared, or you will have a dream featuring a different symbol that somehow reassures you that you have resolved your formerly hidden emotional issue.

Listen to your intuition as you interpret dream symbols. One woman went to sleep with the intention of having a dream that would give her a message about her health. She dreamed of a white bridge-like structure that, upon awakening, she described in her journal. Her intuition told her to notice that it was white and seemed to be flexible. Instead of focusing on what "bridge" might mean, she simply sat with the image, allowing it to suggest a meaning. It occurred to her the message was about the knee pain she had developed that week—that it was related to injuring her connective tissue by not stretching enough before beginning a new exercise. Knowing this, she not only was careful to rest her knee but she also became more mindful of her need to stretch more and listen to her body's signals about overdoing certain movements.

Applying What You Learned to Your Everyday Life

Now that you have learned several expanded-awareness practices for gaining insights into your health and working differently with the archetypal energies affecting them, you need to actually use them. I recommend you work with the practices in this book at least once if not twice a week. You might do a shamanic journey one day and then, a few days later, dialogue with what you encountered. You might do a journaling exercise to identify your current health story and then journey or dialogue, with the intention to learn more about a particular theme such as "resistance" or to learn more about a particular health condition. I encourage you to do all the exercises in this book and regularly use the ones that work best for you.

Connecting with powerful archetypal energies and gaining insights inaccessible to the conscious mind can result in greater motivation, focus, and dedication to writing and bringing to life a new story of your health. Let's say that in working with the archetypal energy of workaholism, you have a dream or a journey in which you encounter a bee—and through dialoguing with it, you come to realize that you are going to be "busy as a bee" and that this has many payoffs for you. You recognize and accept that you don't want to change your "busy bee" nature and simply want a new relationship to it. What comes next? How might you relate to your busy bee nature differently so that it is more beneficial than problematic for you?

Let's say you use a computer all day. You can choose to accept that, yet also find ways to get the movement your body needs to be healthy and find relief from constant mental and visual stimulation. You could commit to doing a short meditation at your desk a few times a day—a meditation in which you focus on your breathing and imagine seeing a still pond and the word "peace." You could also choose to exercise while you are working at your computer, by taking breaks to stretch or lift free weights. You could purchase a mobile device for dictation and communication to get yourself out of your office and into the sunlight and nature when you are writing and recording ideas. When you can, you might walk fast for short bursts and then resume your normal pace. If you watch television, you might stand up and move as you watch.

These are simple changes that can ultimately make a big difference in the story of your health. In fact, according to a 2012 article called "Taking Small Steps Pays Off, Northwestern Health Study Says," which appeared in the *Chicago Tribune,* "small changes in behavior can be the spark needed to make significant strides toward improving general health" and "for long-term success, tracking progress and rewarding small victories helps." [6] Such changes will be easier to make if you accept your workaholism and simply work with it instead of fighting it.

Similarly, you might decide that you're not going to try to cook from scratch on weeknights because, given your working habits, it's an unrealistic goal. You have decided you don't want to change your "busy bee" nature and habits, even though you were ambivalent about them before using expanded-awareness practices and gaining valuable insights. You then decide to hire a meal delivery service or cook ahead on weekends. Once you accept that you do not want to prioritize cooking from scratch each night, you find it easier to admit you need to find other ways to ensure that you eat healthfully. You might realize, too, that you need to be more vigilant about getting a good night's sleep so that you follow through on eating well, exercising, and meditating.

Perhaps the busy bee you dialogued with also reminded you of the importance of working within a community, serving a cause bigger than yourself. This insight might help you to realize that what is troubling you lately and causing you stress isn't actually the amount of work you are doing but the meaning it has for you. A change in the quality or type of work you are doing may help you to work more effectively with your "busy bee" energy. Once again, you can make changes at the margins, perhaps attending a seminar or reading a book that you feel might help you transform your career. Your "busy bee" energy may continue to influence you positively as you shift into spending more time researching ways to make career changes.

Now that you know how to use various practices for gaining insights and for engaging archetypal energies, and you have begun to use these techniques, you might want to explore further what your current health story is, beyond the simple list of problems that we tend to recite at a doctor's office. Your health story has many more components than can be captured in a list.

Next, you will write a new health story so that you can sustain or even improve your current state of wellness. As you begin to do this work, I hope you will pay attention not just to your health challenges but to what is working about your health. Doing so can help you sustain good habits or increase the behaviors that support your health and well-being. At the same time, you will be looking at what you want to experience thematically and energetically—vitality, balance, a feeling of pleasure in your body, and so on. Let the themes you discover suggest specific goals. You might be surprised at how different your goals will look compared to how they would look if you simply made resolutions for improving your health.

CHAPTER FIVE

Write a New Story
of Your Health

Imagine what you would like to experience with your health. Even if your health is reasonably good, you want to be able to maintain that level of health, if not improve on it, in the months and years to come. Let your goal be to write a new health story focused on what you want to experience in the next several years.

If you actually write out your new health story, with paper and pen, it can help you believe that what you aspire to experience can come true. It can also help you affirm what actions you want to take to meet your health goals. However, when it comes to actually bringing your new story of your health to life, you may find you can't sustain positive changes by using willpower alone. The challenge may frustrate you. Hence, I recommend that you write a new story for yourself but also commit to using expanded-awareness practices and journaling to help you bring it to life.

Always remember that you are the storyteller, and you do not have to live according to the dictates of a story written for you by your DNA, your past experiences and actions, or your cultural conditioning. In the last half century or so, we have come to discover that many of the stories we told ourselves can be changed by choices we make. We now know that what we eat and drink, the quality and amount of exercise and movement we get, how well we manage our stress, and our beliefs about illness, aging, and deterioration very much influence our physical health. We can even avoid diseases, illnesses, and accidental injuries by making better, more informed choices and paying attention to small details and changes that can have big effects on our health.

Recently, I was at my dentist's office having my teeth cleaned, and the hygienist told me I was lucky I had a good amount of saliva to keep bacteria from growing on my teeth and underneath my gum line. She mentioned that many people who take common medications experience a side effect of dry mouth, which can lead to bacterial growth, gum disease, loss of teeth, and even cardiovascular disease and diabetes.

I had never considered the importance of something as ordinary as saliva until she brought it up. If I read a medication's list of potential side effects, I might not think "dry mouth" was a serious problem. What if a medication you were on caused this condition and you simply accepted it as bothersome but nothing to worry about? Simply having knowledge can open you to new possibilities, such as finding a different medication or even a different intervention entirely for whatever condition you're treating with drugs. Automatically following doctor's orders and not reflecting on the choices you are making and why you are making them may keep you from writing and bringing to life a better health story.

Health stories will change over time. For example, most of us develop some deterioration in our sense of balance, and we may not realize it until we trip or fall. Choosing to perform movements that can improve balance might prevent an accident that could be serious or have long-term deleterious effects on health, mobility, and outlook. Yet how often do we think about balance before it becomes a problem for us? Writing a new health story can make it more likely that you will not develop a disease or condition in the next several years—as long as you are willing to do the work of transforming your current story.

If you have a chronic condition that is typically irreversible and very difficult to arrest, or you are fighting a life-threatening disease, you might feel there is little you can do other than follow your doctor's orders and hope for the best. But why not write a new and better story for your health that contradicts any dire prognoses based on data and odds?

We know that the power of the mind to affect health is real. All physicians would agree that spontaneous healings do occur. Moreover, through the study of epigenetics, we now understand that our lifestyle choices often have the power to determine whether or not certain genes express themselves in our bodies, reducing or increasing our chances of developing a particular disease.

Recognizing that this is the case, write a new story of your health that is ambitious and inspiring to you. Meanwhile, continue to work with Western medicine—get health screenings and treat conditions—even as you educate yourself about health and wellness, set goals, and establish new habits that promote health and well-being.

Your First Draft of Your Health Story

What will your new health story be? What would you like to experience now and in the future?

Write an initial draft of a new health story for yourself. Use verbs in the present tense and employ "I" language, as if what you were describing were true today—for example, "In my new health story, I am enjoying stamina and good energy as I go about my day," or "In my new health story, I am preparing healthy meals with plenty of vegetables." Later, as you do more of the work in this book and develop deeper insights into what you desire and how you can acquire it, you can refine the story, perhaps adding some details or acknowledging some changes that you want to make, now that you have some new insights. Initially, your health story, written out, might be a few paragraphs long, or as much as a few pages.

As you write, think back to the chapters in your health story you have identified and answered questions about already. Will your new health story include changes in eating habits and resultant weight loss? Greater stamina along with improved moods and a reduced need for pain medication? A better body image, a better relationship to your sexuality, and improved management of hormonal shifts of menopause or andropause? Better management of any conditions you're experiencing, so that you have fewer symptoms? Greater immunity and fewer acute ailments?

What themes do you want to influence your new health story? What title would you like to give it? As you consider the answers, remember that improvements in health can cause improvements in other areas of your life story. You might find that as your health story changes, your confidence is boosted, you have a better relationship with your body and a better self-image, and you are more optimistic and resilient when you face challenges of any sort.

Hidden Aspects of Your Health Story

Even as you are thinking about bringing into being tangible and observable changes in the story of your health, think about your hidden experiences: many health problems begin invisibly, at a cellular level, long before you experience them as physical ailments. Is there anything influencing the development of the pain in your shoulder or back, besides a sedentary lifestyle and hours spent hunched over a computer because of your desk job? Could you be experiencing pain in part because you are "carrying the weight of the world" on your shoulders? Return to the work you did in the previous chapter to shape your new health story and reflect on what you learned.

You might want your new health story to include the activation of innate healing mechanisms and an increase in your immunity. Increasingly, we can access tests that reveal the beginning of biological processes that can lead to illness and disease and track any deterioration. The key to using these tests, in conjunction with techniques for working with archetypal energies, is to recognize your ability to make changes in your health before you experience symptoms.

What if you could arrest or even reverse a condition? In writing a new health story for yourself, you might include aspirations to see better results the next time you do laboratory tests. For example, you might hope to see reduced inflammation or tumor size, more stable blood sugar levels over time, improved T-cell levels (a measure of immune response), or better levels of certain vitamins or minerals. (Note: All of these tests can be ordered by a physician, and some can be self-ordered direct through a mail-order lab without a prescription.)

If you seem to be developing a condition, remember that overtreatment can lead to other problems. For example, all surgery has its risks, so even if you have a procedure scheduled, you might want to work on alleviating the condition that will be addressed surgically. There are no guarantees, of course, but writing a new health story in which you avoid surgery yet overcome pain or a particular unhealthy condition—such as a blood clot or blockage—might help.

Your new health story might include a statement such as "I work with techniques for breaking up the blockage in my artery, and I achieve success, eliminating the need for surgery." Even if that does not feel true for you in the moment, write it out anyway. Again, you can always craft a new draft of your health story later. Remember, however, not to ignore your doctor's advice. I suggest you employ the strategy I did when I had a blockage in my kidney. After using expanded-awareness practices to reduce the blockage, I asked my physician to repeat the test that had revealed the blockage, just in case it had cleared and I didn't need surgery after all.

The Benefits of an Optimistic Approach

How realistic or optimistic should you be in writing your new health story? As reported by Anne Teregesen in the October 19, 2015, edition of the *Wall Street Journal,* "Over the past two decades, dozens of studies from psychologists, medical doctors and neuroscientists have shown that older people with more negative views of aging fare more poorly on health than those with less-pessimistic attitudes." She goes on to note that studies that are controlled for education levels, socioeconomic status, and health status show that people who are negative or pessimistic about aging have worse memory, are more likely to develop cardiac disease as well as to die younger (on average, 7.5 years earlier), and are less likely to eat healthfully, exercise, and recover from a severe disability.[1] My suggestion is to be as optimistic as possible when you write your new health story.

You might incorporate into it a statement such as "While it once seemed impossible, I now have the stamina to work full days most of the time," or "Despite my fears that I wouldn't be able to maintain an exercise program, I was able to do so and lost 35 pounds, keeping it off."

When you have written your new health story on paper, you might want to begin working with your unconscious to learn more so that you can further refine your story. Regularly interacting with your unconscious through expanded-awareness practices may lead you to more readily catch yourself acting in ways that contradict the new health story you have chosen to write for yourself.

With new insights and wisdom from your unconscious guiding you, it can be easier to make better choices in the moment, and overall. For example, you might overcome any fear of offending a healer you have been working with who is not helping you as much as you had hoped, and find the courage to frankly confront that person to get information that will help you decide whether to continue the relationship.

You might discover that your resistance to speaking to your doctor about how he or she is interacting with you has a lot to do with themes playing out in other areas of your life. By altering your relationship to archetypal energies such as "the wise king" or "authority figures," you could make it easier to speak freely to the healer you are working with and make the right choice about whether to continue your partnership. It could become easier for you to confront your doctor when you are uncomfortable with how you are being spoken to (for example, if your physician seems to judge you for needing clearer explanations).

Although the work ahead of you may seem daunting at times, remember that changes at the margins are important and they have a cumulative effect. You can always improve your health to some degree simply through making better choices and taking action one small step at a time toward replacing your old habits. Add goals for healthier habits to your new health story.

Do You Need to Do Research?

As you begin to write a new story of your health, you may realize you have some research to do. Gathering and considering information provided by experts in the fields of nutrition, exercise, psychology, or stress reduction may be in order. You might also research ways to get more healthy movement, and incorporate into your new health story a vision of yourself engaging in that type of movement. If you don't know what type of diet would work best for you, learn more about different types of dietary approaches. Then, use the expanded-awareness exercises you find in this book to deepen your inquiry.

Researching which interventions and approaches are available is a good idea, but keep in mind that everyone's body is unique. As Mark Hyman, MD, a leader in the field of functional medicine, wrote in his book *The UltraMind Solution,* "Your individual genetic makeup determines what you need to be optimally healthy."[2]

Diets that work well for people who are physiologically different from you—for example, older or younger, male and not female, of European rather than Asian descent—might not work well for you. If you are not comfortable with your level of flexibility, you can try yoga, but you may find there are some forms of yoga that are a better fit for you than others.

Do You Need to Research Assistive Devices?

As you write your new health story, notice your attitudes about sexuality, body image, and using assistive devices such as hearing aids and a cane or leg brace to manage symptoms and conditions that are permanent or temporary. Perhaps you are uncomfortable wearing devices that are obviously designed to make up for physical deficits. Researching them may open your mind to using them. You might have fears about undergoing procedures or surgeries commonly associated with your condition, disease, or situation, yet there might be more nonsurgical options than you thought. For example, you might be able to manage your symptoms of foot pain through orthotics and/or Pilates foot exercises and avoid surgery. In doing research, you might discover there are ways to treat your ailments without using pharmaceutical drugs.

Could There Be New Interventions You Have Not Heard Of?

Could there be some tests you do not know about that might help you monitor a condition, so that you don't feel forced to make a difficult decision about treatment right now? Often, having a way to monitor a condition can help reduce your fears about it quickly getting worse and causing a health crisis.

I've had an enlarged prostate for many years. It had been increasingly impacting my life, yet I was not willing to risk having to suffer the side effects of some of the common medications or surgeries for treating it. I was considering a procedure to shrink my prostate that has been deemed experimental, and was told that I had to be in a clinical trial to get it, so I decided to try to be enrolled in the trial. To qualify, I needed to be cancer free, so I underwent a biopsy of my prostate. As it turns out, I was diagnosed with prostate cancer. Mine is a slow-growth cancer and, following my doctor's advice, I am going to watch and wait rather than treat it aggressively. While I can't be part of the clinical trial, I was able to get the new procedure anyway—a procedure I would not have known about had I not done research into other options beyond the traditional drugs and surgery.

I continue to use energy healing techniques to learn more, to further shrink my prostate and to eradicate the cancer. I am regularly visualizing my energetic immune system absorbing any diseased parts of my prostate and then carrying them outside my body into the earth. In doing so, and working with sacred space as I use this technique, I honor the power I have to connect with the energies of the invisible worlds for my healing.

I am getting all the information I can from my Western medicine doctors so I can know my options. I continue to be open-minded and optimistic about my health story. The results of PSA (prostate-specific antigen) tests my physician and I are using to monitor my cancer have reinforced my belief that the healing work I am doing is helping me maintain or even improve my condition.

Do You Need to Research Any Tests You Have Had or Might Want to Have Done?

Because of the risk of overtreatment after receiving certain test results, it's important to understand the limitations of testing and how tests can be used to make decisions. It's also important to access the hidden wisdom of your unconscious to know which health choices might be the best for you as a unique individual.

For example, many women understandably fear developing breast cancer but are also concerned about the tests for it. If you are a woman who is deciding whether to take a test that would show if you have variations on the BRCA1 or BRCA2 genes, which predispose you to developing breast cancer, what would you do with the information if the test results were positive? Also, many women are concerned and confused about new guidance about mammogram screenings for what has been called stage 0 cancer, or ductal carcinoma in situ (DCIS). When looked at in populations of women, early mammogram screenings clearly lead to overtreatment in many cases. However, when a woman considers her *personal* risk for stage 0 cancer turning into cancer, it can be difficult for her to decide whether she wants to get a screening mammogram, and what she wants to do if diagnosed with DCIS.

Knowing more about the pros and cons of screening mammograms, breast biopsies, and treatments for ductal carcinoma in situ, and getting a second opinion (perhaps from another physician or lab reading the results) can help a woman write a new story for her health that she feels is right for her. In addition, working with her unconscious can help her gain insights into how she can positively affect her breast health at the cellular level. This can help her to have greater clarity in working with her physician to make the right choice for her about tests and screenings.

A woman in this situation may also want to try to reverse or halt the condition on her own, using her inner healer, before undergoing more tests.[3] Balancing healing work with screening, tests, and lifestyle changes supportive of wellness can be a part of a satisfying new health story, even if there is a health condition or concern.

It can also be difficult for men to decide whether to be screened for prostate cancer when they have no symptoms because they may be opening themselves up to overtreatment. In fact, even when they have been diagnosed with prostate cancer, increasingly, some men are doing what I am doing: taking a wait-and-see approach instead of getting surgery because this particular cancer is often slow to develop.[4]

Do You Need to Research Costs of Tests, Treatments, and Other Supports for a Better Health Story?

Cost may be a factor in what you imagine yourself experiencing in your new health story. Again, research might help you discover options you had not thought about—for example, getting dental work done at a dental school or using a different provider or working with a different healer. A wait-and-see approach can make sense in some cases.

Let's say you know your dental fillings are well worn, but you are keeping those teeth bacteria-free. You are only risking a broken filling and an emergency trip to the dentist if you wait. However, if you are in need of a knee or hip replacement, the weakened joint could break, causing a dangerous fall. In this case, you would need to be more aggressive about researching your options so that you get the replacement sooner rather than later. In consultation with our health care providers and inner healers, we need to balance the risk of not treating an illness with the risks of prematurely doing so.

Have You Researched the Costs of "Overdoing It"?

You may have adopted new health practices that in and of themselves are good, but perhaps you have become somewhat obsessive about them, rendering them harmful in some ways. What is the cost of overdoing exercise, or being too rigid about your new, healthier diet? For starters, the pressure you put on yourself to be perfect might create so much stress that you are lowering your immunity. Also, when it comes to some forms of exercise, you may need to be more mindful about their potential to lead to injury. What is the cost of continuing to do yoga if you are having joint problems? What is the cost of juicing and consuming very large quantities of kale, which affects levels of thyroid hormones?[5]

If you are obsessing about a particular health regimen, you may be neglecting other heath practices that would benefit you. For example, you may be eating better but continuing to get inadequate sleep—and not realizing how important sleep is to your health. In the sphere of exercise, you may be emphasizing one activity over others that are important—for example, focusing on aerobic activity and neglecting strength, flexibility, and balance. Working with your unconscious might help you discover that you are putting too much focus on some habits or aspects of your health and not enough on others.

Discovering the Origins of Your Health Habits and Choices

In looking at the first draft of your new health story, think about the origins of your behaviors. The health habits that you take for granted may be rooted in beliefs that are not true to your values.

How much have others influenced your ideas about how you should act? Who told you to always clean your plate, to fear gaining weight and losing your attractiveness, or to keep a stiff upper lip when you are in pain? Did you take to heart statements your parents, teachers, or romantic partners made casually or thoughtlessly, such as "In our family, everyone dies young," or "We all suffer from depression because it runs in the family. It's just the way we are"? Have you internalized cultural messages you consciously reject?

You may wish to journey to the lower world (instructions can be found in Chapter Four: Expanded-Awareness Practices for Gaining Insights and Energy), if you haven't already, to discover the origins of your beliefs as well as your habits. Knowing where they came from can help you feel less ambivalent about transforming them. For example, if their origins lie in a fear of displeasing someone whose approval you sought, you may come to realize your fear is irrational, which can help you let go of it. If your long-gone parents instilled in you the belief that you should be embarrassed to admit you are hurting and need help, and that belief is interfering with your getting the support you need to change the story of your health, you may be ready to reject it.

As you work with the expanded-awareness practices to become more conscious of hidden influences on your health story, you are likely to begin recognizing your role in writing it. You can start to see what you are doing, perhaps unconsciously, to bring about events and situations you might not like. It is easy to blame genetics, a family legacy of disease or poor habits, or external pressures for making choices that are out of synch with your intention to bring to life a better health story.

By continuing to be more aware of your thoughts and actions, and by working with archetypal energies and dialoguing with them, you may find that your excuses for not being able to change your health story more easily fall away. You may find you are able to go beyond merely using your willpower to make small changes at the margins; you may even be able to make radical changes to your health story. As you get more practice in being honest with yourself about your role in writing the health story you have had until now, your confidence in your ability to write a new and better one may grow. Subsequently, it will be easier for you to face uncomfortable truths about choices you have made.

Embodying Your New Health Story

Once you have written a first draft for a new story of your health, try the following exercise. It can help you discover whether your new health story feels right for you. If it does not, you can explore why it doesn't, and decide whether to make changes in it or try to bring your new health story to life, even if it may feel overly ambitious to you now.

To prepare for the practice, reread the new health story you just wrote. Set your intention to imagine you have brought that story to life and are experiencing a typical day for you. Next, open sacred space, cleanse your energy field, and do mindful breathing so you are ready to use the practice.

EXPANDED-AWARENESS PRACTICE: IMAGINE YOU INHABIT YOUR NEW HEALTH STORY

Imagine you are experiencing the new health story you wrote. Notice how you feel as you picture the beginning of your typical day. How do you feel as you awaken? Where are you? How do you feel as you begin your everyday activities?

How do you feel in your body? What emotions do you experience when you look in the mirror? What do you see as you look at yourself?

Now imagine yourself engaged in an activity you value (working, socializing, and so forth). How do you feel in your body? Let the scene unfold before you and fade into a new scene of you enjoying an activity.

Remember, you are experiencing the new health story you wrote for yourself, not the one you have been living according to up until this point.

What is happening in this scene? How do you feel in your body? Are you able to do things you weren't able to do before? What are they?

In this new health story, what do you see yourself doing differently?

- Have you found a new way to deal with ailments that are common for you?
- Are you free from pain or discomfort?
- Do you feel good in your body as it is?
- What are you eating and drinking?
- Are you sleeping differently?
- Have your moods changed?
- Are you doing different activities?
- Are you moving more?
- Are you thinner or more muscular or toned?
- Are you more flexible physically? What does that look like for you?
- Do you have more stamina? How is that affecting your activities?
- Do you move more confidently and feel better about yourself?
- Are you dressed differently—and if so, why?
- Now imagine that you are sitting down to a meal. What are you eating?
- Is it different from what you used to eat?
- What sorts of snacks do you have on hand now?
- What has changed about your eating?

Observe any changes from what you experience now in your real life. Do you feel different emotions or have a different attitude as you live according to this new story and go about your daily activities?

Continue until you feel you have seen what you need to see and experienced what you need to experience. Let your intuition guide you in deciding when to end this exercise.

After you have returned to ordinary consciousness, close sacred space. When you have finished this exercise, journal about what you experienced and learned. How does this new health story feel to you? Can you accept it as is, even if it feels a little too optimistic? Are you willing to stick with it?

How will you be different when you live out this new story of your health? Will you be more assertive, more peaceful, more playful, more confident, or something else? Imagine you inhabit your new health story and will be able to pick up on any discomfort you may have with it. Remember that if you are unsure of whether you are completely happy with this new health story you have written, you can always modify it later. In Chapter Eight: Revising the Story of Your Health, you can go deeper into reviewing your health story and revising it, if you like. You might find that once you have achieved certain goals, you want to write a new health story that incorporates even more habits for fostering good health. Or, you might find that you want to revise your health story to be more realistic for you if, despite many attempts to bring the new one to life, you are not making the progress you had hoped.

For now, however, why not affirm your new health story and infuse it with your intention to bring it into being? Try reading it aloud from your journal, while looking in the mirror and making eye contact with yourself as much as possible. Then, when you are finished, smile at yourself. Several of my workshop participants have reported that when they smile, they feel different almost instantly—sometimes, they even feel pain subside. Possibly, this is because smiling instantly creates endorphins, hormones that make us feel happy, which can make it easier to be optimistic. You might want to simply look in the mirror daily and smile as part of a ritual or habit designed to affirm your new health story.

Notice how you feel whenever you affirm what you will experience in your new health story, rereading it or reciting it aloud, with or without looking in a mirror. Do the statements you wrote feel true for you? Do you feel a sense of doubt or resistance? If so, try saying these statements aloud again a few times to see if your feelings change. If they don't, consider using some of the practices in this book to better understand your doubts and resistance.

Express Your New Health Story
Through the Arts

You might want to express your new health story through the arts. Why not write a song or a poem that captures it, or dance in a way that expresses it? You might draw or paint a picture or create a sculpture that represents what your new health story will be when you are living according to it.

When you are struggling with health symptoms or worried that your health story will not play out as you want it to, you might want to sing your song, read your poem aloud, or dance to express what you would like to experience health-wise. If you make a picture or sculpture that is evocative of your new story of health, pay attention to any new perspectives you gain by looking at it and contemplating it.

Synchronicities and Messages about Your Health

Although using the practices in this book will help you to better understand the story of your health, and to write a new and more satisfying one, you can also gain insights and wisdom from Source simply by remaining open to synchronicities. A synchronicity could be a chance encounter with a person who happens to know exactly where you can find a particular type of healer you are looking for, a book with useful health advice that catches your eye unexpectedly, or a story you happen to come across that seems to call to you to check it out because it has value for you. The synchronicity could be a snippet of conversation or a lyric of a recorded song being played right when you need to hear that message. It could be an image that has meaning for you that shows up on a poster or magazine cover when you are sitting in a doctor's office, traveling to visit a health clinic, or simply going about your daily life and hoping to get clarity about a health decision you have to make.

Synchronicities often appear when you are observing nature. Pay attention if the same type of insect, bird, or animal appears before you and you sense it has meaning for you. It may appear in specific circumstances, such as whenever you start doubting your ability to live according to your new health story or are wrestling with whether to discontinue a particular health habit, question or investigate a medication, or change healers. Listen to your instincts about messages that come to you in a synchronistic way. You might dialogue with the messages or the messengers.

Shamans often look to nature for guidance and messages from Source, and many Jungian techniques can be adapted for use in nature, as you will see. Working outdoors to access insights and energies hidden in the unconscious can yield many benefits and advantages. Let's look next at the many ways in which you can interact with nature in order to write and bring to life a new story for your health.

CHAPTER SIX

Nature's Healing Effects

As you write and refine a new story of your health and begin to bring it to life, it can be invaluable to explore your relationship to nature and work with nature. Because we evolved to experience nature as our home, it makes sense that being outdoors among the trees, plants, and animals fosters physical, mental, and emotional well-being. In fact, Richard Louv, author of *The Nature Principle* and *Last Child in the Woods,* suggests that our exposure to nature is so important to our overall health that we should think of it as "vitamin N." Incorporating nature into your life more often, in a variety of ways, may help you improve your health story—and even the overall story of your life.

Carl Jung said that the earth has a soul, and the shamans I have met would agree. Indigenous healers in Peru speak of Pachamama, Mother Earth, as the source of all healing. And within that spiritual entity known as Mother Earth, they say there are entities with consciousness of their own. These spirits include not just human beings but, as psychotherapist Edward Tick, PhD, describes it, "all creatures, natural beings, and processes—animals, plants, stones, clothing, colors, and the weather—have spirits with which we can communicate."[1]

Whatever your spiritual beliefs and your ideas about shared and individual consciousness, when you reconnect with nature, you might experience that you have a relationship with the consciousness I call Source. You might even shape that relationship to make it a reciprocal one, as you observe and engage nature while it observes and engages you. Some say nature is God's creation, and others say nature is Spirit expressing itself. Whatever your beliefs about nature and Spirit, we do know that being in nature has many benefits for health and well-being. Working with it actively, using expanded-awareness practices, may be especially helpful for improving your health story.

Nature's Recalibrating Effects

Scientists and shamans alike know that all of life is woven into a web of infinite connections, contributing to the larger whole in a system that is complex beyond our imagining. When we sit quietly at the edge of a lake, or hike through a wildflower-strewn meadow, or walk through a cool, dark forest, we quickly become aware of our unity with the natural world. We fall back into natural rhythms—rhythms we are no longer in synch with as a result of living by the clock and spending much of our time in man-made spaces lit by electricity. Nature has a way of recalibrating us and helping us gain a new perspective on our stressors so that they seem less overwhelming.

A man named Brendan reported that he had been excessively worrying about his health conditions. Although he was healthy, he had been imagining he might have or be developing a serious disease. Brendan's frequent brooding about this possibility was causing him mental and emotional stress, which he was trying to reduce by doing shamanic journeying and spending time in nature. As a result, he was beginning to develop a different attitude toward his health and his fears about it.

One day, he was waiting for the results of some lab tests from his doctor, and Brendan was nervous because he had not heard anything yet from his physician. When he went to his doctor's office to find out what was going on, the nurse he consulted said she had to check with the doctor. Brendan felt she was putting off talking to him because the results must have been bad and she wanted to avoid being the one to tell him. All of this was very distressing. Brendan went outside and was drawn to a particular tree. He began to silently communicate with it, connecting to its energy. Very shortly, he felt less anxious and gained a new perspective. He began to see how he was creating health concerns in his mind but was not necessarily experiencing them in his body.

Brendan was able to step back from his worries and recognize them for what they were: irrational fears he could assert power over. In particular, being present with the tree, communing with it, was very healing for him and reduced the intensity of his fears even before he knew what his medical test results were. (As it turned out, they were normal.) All of these realizations came about simply because he stepped outside, consciously chose to work with the energy of a tree, and opened himself up to receiving its energy and the insights it offered him.

If you haven't considered nature's effects on your health and well-being, you might want to do the following journaling exercise to help you think more about ways you have worked with nature that have helped you in the past.

JOURNALING EXERCISE: NATURE AND YOUR HEALTH

Reflect on the questions below, and answer them in your journal. In fact, you may wish to write your answers either sitting outdoors or indoors looking through a window at a beautiful, natural scene.

- What connections do you see between spending time in nature and enjoying better health?
- In what physical spaces do you feel most vibrant, energized, contented, and healthy? Do these spaces have natural elements, or are they, perhaps, in nature itself? Are there specific natural spaces that have such a positive effect on your sense of well-being that you would consider them your favorite spaces? What are they, and why do you feel such a connection to them?
- Do you spend as much time as you would like in nature? If not, why is that?
- What is it about nature that you crave? For example, do you get enough sunlight, time spent near or in water or woods, time touching the earth, grass, trees, and so forth?
- How do you feel in your body when you are in natural spaces, such as the woods, a lake, a river, the ocean, or your backyard? How do you feel emotionally in these spaces? Consider various natural spaces you have been in, as you answer this question. You may find that you feel different in another type of natural space, for instance, in a dark, quiet forest versus a sunny meadow.
- Are there any ways in which not being in nature benefits you? For example, are you trying to avoid allergens outdoors or extremes in temperature?

- When it comes to achieving a satisfying amount of time in nature, what has worked for you in the past? How might you get past obstacles such as outdoor allergens or extremes in temperature to spend more time enjoying nature?

  For example, is there a nature center you could visit where you could get breaks from the heat or warm up between forays into the snow? How might you make time for being in nature?
- What is the story of the relationship between nature and your sense of well-being? Is there an anecdote that captures your relationship? If so, write about it. Give it a title. Do you feel it has a theme, and if so, what is it?

The Evidence for Nature's Healing Powers

Many people have intuited that nature has healing powers, but now researchers are discovering more about how our bodies and minds benefit from our interactions with nature. When it comes to scientific and medical research, some of the positive effects of nature are measured using the self-reporting of participants in the studies. Others are measured by lower blood pressure or lower levels of stress hormones such as cortisol. Some studies look at brain activity changes, which show we have a different internal experience when we are exposed to nature. These experiences contribute to better mental and physical health in the short and long term.

A 2007 British study showed a walk in nature reduced depression in 71 percent of the participants.[2] That matches up with Japanese research into the practice of *shinrin-yoku*, which can be translated as "forest bathing," or immersion in a wooded environment. Studies have shown that walking in the woods lowers levels of the stress hormones cortisol, adrenaline, and noradrenaline, boosting immunity and mood. It also reduces heart rate, lowers blood pressure, improves sleep, and increases anticancer protein levels.[3]

Eva M. Selhub and Alan C. Logan have pointed out in their book *Your Brain on Nature: The Science of Nature's Influence on Your Health, Happiness and Vitality* that, in England and America, the Victorians sent those with "nervous conditions" or tuberculosis to sanitariums. These facilities were typically located in pine forests, as evergreen trees were believed to emit something into the air that promoted healing. As it turns out, these claims were not the mere invention of imaginative promoters of sanitariums. Selhub and Logan note, "Natural chemicals secreted by evergreen trees, collectively known as phytoncide, have also been associated with improvements in the activity of our frontline immune defenders."[4] The air in natural areas, especially in forests or near moving waters such as rivers, tends to have a very high concentration of negative ions, known to increase levels of the mood-boosting neurotransmitter serotonin. These types of ions also are associated with a sense of greater vitality, and they reduce depression, fatigue, and stress.[5] Breathing them in is easy to do when we are outdoors in nature.

Touching soil, or perhaps just being near it and breathing it in to some degree, benefits health, too. An increasing amount of research is showing a connection between microbes, encountered when outdoors, and a healthy gut colony of organisms that contributes to digestive health and even positive moods and protection from depression and anxiety. Dirt puts us in contact with microorganisms that establish their home in our digestive system. As David Perlmutter, MD, wrote in his book *Brain Maker:* "The microbiome is dynamic. It's ever-changing in response to our environment—the air we breathe, the people we touch, the drugs we take, the dirt and germs we encounter, the things we consume, and even the thoughts we have. Just as food gives our bodies information, so does our gut bacteria speak to our DNA, our biology, and ultimately, our longevity."[6] A healthy colony of microbes in our gut serves to promote our immunity as well as healthy cognitive abilities and emotional well-being.

Gardening is one outdoor activity known to have many health benefits, including reduction of physical pain and stress, improved mental wellness, increased physical fitness, increased social contact and sense of community, and greater consumption of fruits and vegetables.[7] In a garden, you are exposed to sunlight, needed for the production of vitamin D and serotonin. Both affect mood, reducing the risk of depression. Most of our serotonin, a neurotransmitter that contributes to a sense of contentment and happiness, is produced not in the brain, where it is used, but in our digestive system, where microorganisms from the environment live. It makes sense that being in the sunlight, touching dirt, and getting physical activity could improve depression and anxiety. Then too, planting, weeding, and harvesting vegetables in a garden offers the health benefit of greater accessibility to foods known to promote health.

One of my clients, who had cancer, told me that gardening made her feel happy and relaxed because it made her feel connected to the earth and life itself. She also said it made her less preoccupied with her cancer.

Although being in nature, enjoying it and moving our bodies as we appreciate it, is good for the body and mind, we are increasingly spending time indoors in artificial environments. Consequently, our eyes and skin are exposed to artificial light. We know that interaction with technological devices affects our eyesight. It's now common to have an eyeglass prescription for close reading, one for regular vision including distance vision, and yet another for reading from a computer screen or mobile device located 20 to 26 inches from our eyes (trifocals are common now, too). Children who spend more time indoors have an increased risk of nearsightedness. Researchers are still looking into how indoor lighting might be affecting us differently from how natural sunlight affects us. Fluorescent lighting, for example, may increase your chances of developing an eye disease or cataracts.[8]

Being indoors or in an urban setting, away from natural sounds and exposed to more mechanistic sounds created by humans, has deleterious health effects as well. According to a report issued by the Harvard School of Public Health in conjunction with the John A. Volpe National Transportation Systems Center, "Excessive anthropogenic [caused by humans] noise has been associated with annoyance, disruption of sleep and cognitive processes, hearing impairment, and adverse impacts on cardiovascular and endocrine systems."[9] It seems the further away from nature we get, the more our bodies have to struggle to adjust to our unnatural lifestyles. Consider whether this struggle may be related to health problems you are experiencing.

Why are we so sensitive to the difference between natural and unnatural environments? How could something as simple as unnatural sounds have such strong effects on our emotional well-being and health? The answers may lie in how the body, brain, and nervous system process experiences in man-made environments versus natural environments. One benefit of spending time in nature is that you enter a mind state similar to the one typically achieved when using shamanic practices, and the nervous system is able to switch from an alert sympathetic state (fight or flight) to a soothing, restorative parasympathetic state (rest and digest) for better health. That switchover fosters greater immunity and triggers a process of cellular repair in the body.

Research on "green exercise"—in other words, exercise undertaken outdoors, in a natural area—shows it provides even greater health benefits than exercise indoors, presumably because of the effects of nature. Exercising near water may be especially advantageous.

In his book *Blue Mind: The Surprising Science That Shows How Being Near, In, On, or Under Water Can Help Make You Happier, Healthier, and More Connected at What You Do,* author Wallace J. Nichols cites many neuroscience studies showing that our moods can be positively affected by time spent interacting with bodies of water. He suggests we humans evolved to be calmed by the mere sight of water before us—a patch of blue meeting the sky and above a field of green.

Perhaps we have inherited an ancestral memory of walking across a lush green landscape, rich with plants that feed us and the animals, and looking toward the horizon to be comforted by the sight of the nourishing waters of a lake or river. In such places, we may experience a sense of home as well as a connection to the land that helps us to better understand who we are and what our lives are about. Writing in *Walden; or, Life in the Woods,* Henry David Thoreau said, "A lake is the landscape's most beautiful and expressive feature. It is earth's eye; looking into which the beholder measures the depth of his own nature." [10]

Communicating and Communing with Nature

Recognize that simply being in or near nature can bring you information about your health and be "medicine" for you in ways you might not expect—as my client, Brendan, came to see when he stood quietly and made a connection with a tree while waiting to receive health test results. As you observe a snowfall through the window of a quiet room, you might feel moved to dialogue with the experience and let it inform you about your health. You may get a message about purity, innocence, freshness, or a new beginning. You might realize you need to slow down and be less distracted. Even if you only intended to sit for a while and observe the snow falling, you might begin to realize you and your health are part of a larger whole of nature and that remembering this truth will help you experience greater wellness.

One winter evening, I took a walk and was looking at a waxing moon, which was about half full. It would appear and disappear in the sky, as the clouds passed in front of it. I paused to interact and dialogue with it to discover what it could teach me about my health story. I was reminded of how some things can be present but not visible—things that contribute to poor health and to good health. I understood that if I intend to see them, and I remain vigilant, I can catch glimpses of the invisible world and the wisdom it holds for me. Soon after this, I was diagnosed with prostate cancer, which was present but not visible, just like the moon behind the cloud.

Taking advantage of opportunities to reconnect with nature and its elements can give you insights and energies for healing. Even if you may have seen many snowfalls or thunderstorms in your life, you might want to pause the next time you experience one. Open yourself to what it might bring you—messages, a renewed feeling of gratitude, or something else. I also suggest that when you use expanded-awareness practices in nature, you consider beginning by opening sacred space, cleansing your energy field, and doing mindful breathing, and then closing sacred space afterward. Should you receive any messages from the snow, rain, sky, clouds, or ground, consider thanking them, as this shows respect for the wisdom of nature.

If it has been a while since you have spent time in nature, connecting to its healing powers, you might want to do the following simple expanded-awareness practice, which can help you connect with the energy of the sun. Do you long to feel its rays upon your skin? In writing about an indigenous African ritual for greeting the sunrise, Carl Jung said, "The longing for light is the longing for consciousness."[11]

When was the last time you made a point of watching a sunrise? What are you missing by taking for granted that since the sun will rise again tomorrow, you can always catch a sunrise some other day?

The following simple expanded-awareness practice requires no preparation other than planning to find a place to greet the sun as it rises.

EXPANDED-AWARENESS PRACTICE: SUN GREETING

Plan to awaken before dawn to watch the sunrise in a natural area where you can fully appreciate the experience with an unobstructed view. As soon as you can upon arising, go outside to greet the sun as it begins to spread light upward from the horizon, filling the sky.

Be fully present as you soak in its light and warmth. Imagine it is observing and greeting you, just as you are observing and greeting it.

Become mindful of your breathing. Then, as you face the east, salute the sun, adopting whatever posture feels right to you.

You might want to do a yoga pose such as the sun salutation, or you can simply extend your arms out to your side, with your palms up, and thrust your chest forward.

Open yourself up to the sun's energy. Look out at the horizon or sky and then close your eyes so you can turn your face fully toward the sun. Notice the sensation of your breathing and the sensation of the sun as it strikes your skin and its light penetrates your eyelids.

Try not to consciously create thoughts about what is happening; simply be present to the experience, and continue to focus on your breath. You might open your eyes and watch the changing colors of the sky, but do not directly gaze at the sun, as this can damage your eyes.

Ask the sun, "What message do you have for me about my health?" Wait for the answer. Be open to the form of the answer. It may simply be an inner knowing, or it may be a word or an image that comes to you.

Ask the sun, "What do I need to release to help me live according to a better health story?" Ask it, too, what you need to bring in for that purpose. You might also ask, "What in me needs to be nourished so that it may grow?" Each time, wait for an answer before posing the next question.

When you sense it is the right time to end your ritual of interaction with the energy of the sun, open your eyes. Thank the sun for its messages and energy.

After you have used this practice, journal about it. Did you receive any insights that you found helpful? What was it like for you to have this experience?

Expanded-awareness practices such as this one can be used to work co-creatively with the energies in nature, accessing their healing properties. If you do not get a clear, direct answer to your inquiries about your health when you are in nature and trying to communicate with it, remain present to the experience and simply observe what you are feeling and sensing. Later, you can choose to do a dialogue and learn more.

The following expanded-awareness practice, to be done out in nature, is a technique for tapping into the wisdom of the unconscious mind. It is similar to the Jungian sand tray technique and Native American sand paintings created for healing purposes by people of the Navajo, Zuni, Hopi, and Plains tribes, but here I am calling it a "nature painting" because it might not involve sand as one of its elements.

The nature painting will serve as a symbolic representation of the information about your health that your inner healer has to share with you. It might show you that you are putting all your efforts into addressing one area of your health while neglecting another. It might reveal that you lack trust in your own judgment and wisdom about what health treatments and practices are working well for you. These are just two examples of what you might discover while working with this exercise.

To gain insights into your health, formulate a question you would like answered. It could be "What is the current story of my health?" or "What am I not seeing about my health situation?" or "What is the cause of my digestive problems returning?"

Go to a natural area where you won't be disturbed, whether it is a park, beach, or backyard. If you can't access and work with a natural area outdoors where you will have privacy, you might do the exercise indoors. In that case, you would use sticks, flowers, shells, stones, leaves, and so on that you have been drawn to and have gathered, and a tabletop or floor on which you could do your nature painting.

Whether you are outdoors or indoors when using this practice, I suggest you start by opening sacred space, cleansing your energy field, and doing mindful breathing. When you are ready, begin the exercise.

EXPANDED-AWARENESS PRACTICE: NATURE PAINTING

After formulating a question you would like answered, draw a circle on the ground using a stick or your finger, or create a circle using natural objects you find nearby. Look for more natural objects—perhaps a particular stone or fallen leaf—and arrange them within the circle that serves as your canvas. Let your intuition guide you in what items you choose to make a part of your "painting" and where you place the objects.

Continue until you feel you have completed the painting. Sit or stand, looking at your creation. Notice what insights come up for you as you observe it and contemplate it.

You might want to dialogue with some aspect of the nature painting to get further insights—or dialogue with it further at a later point. If you feel your nature painting has a healing energy for you, you can use your hands to sweep its energy into your energy field.

When you feel you are ready to end this experience of connecting with nature and your unconscious, thank the energies of nature for assisting you.

After you feel you have completed your work with your nature painting, close sacred space (if you opened it) and make sure you return the objects to nature. Journal about your experiences. Here are some questions you might answer:

- How did you pick the spot you chose? What made it appealing to you?
- What did you observe when choosing and placing objects?
- At what point did you feel you had completed your painting? Why do you think that felt to you like a completion point?
- What did your nature painting show you about your health? What insights do you have as a result of using it?

Note that you may wish to take a photograph of your painting before you return the objects to nature. More insights might arise later when you look at the image.

A variation on this practice is to leave the nature painting where it is and return to the spot a few days later, or perhaps several times. Notice whether the air, animals, people, or water may have moved some of the objects in your painting. If so, observe what has changed and how you feel about the changes. Notice what insights and emotions come up for you as you look at the altered nature painting. Dialogue with the painting or your feelings, if you feel moved to do so. Again, if you feel your nature painting has a healing energy for you, you might want to use your hands to sweep that into your energy field. If you opened sacred space, be sure to close it—and return the objects to where you found them. As always, journal about your experience afterward.

Nature paintings can offer you many insights into your health itself—such as the origin of your recent fatigue or difficulties you are having with accepting the changes in your body that are a result of dealing with your medical condition. You can also use the nature painting technique to gain information and guidance about other questions regarding your health story—for example, working with a particular healer with whom you are partnering.

If you have a question about working with a particular healer, be sure not to symbolically represent that person in your painting. Doing so might interfere with that person's energy in some way, and may hinder you from connecting with your own emotional responses to and hidden beliefs about the healer that the other person isn't responsible for. Instead, ask a question such as "What do I need to know about partnering with this healer at this time?" and allow the objects, chosen by your unconscious mind, to reveal what you are not consciously aware of, and to suggest what actions you might want to take.

For example, you might discover you are uncomfortable with the healer you have partnered with because you see him or her as lacking empathy for you, but the painting might suggest to you that you are projecting onto this person your own need for self-compassion. You might realize you want to work with this healer, and you can accept a less-than-ideal "bedside manner" and lack of emotional response to you, but you need to take time to nurture yourself emotionally and give yourself credit for your hard work at managing your condition.

A woman named Emily wanted to discover why she was experiencing abdominal bloating, so she did a nature painting on a beach. It incorporated some stones in a line from the bottom of the circle to the middle, and at the end of the line, she placed a broken piece of white plastic from a lighter. She interpreted this to mean there was an unnatural blockage somewhere in her digestive system, so she went to a massage therapist who massaged her belly, releasing gas and alleviating the bloating and discomfort. Emily then began to pay attention to her belly to see if the gas and bloating returned, and later traced the condition to a food she was eating, which she decided to cut out of her diet. While she had bought it at a natural foods store, she discovered when reading the label that it had more unnatural ingredients than she had thought. Emily intuited that she had been drawn to the piece of plastic, the only unnatural item in her nature painting, because on some level, she knew she was experiencing gastrointestinal distress due to something unnatural that had blocked her digestive tract.

You might observe the individual pieces in your nature painting, and where you placed them, and the positions nature moved them to (if you leave the painting and come back to it), and gain any number of insights about what is going on in your health story.

Let's say you notice that an object you realize represented your fatigue was moved by the wind, or perhaps animals, closer to the center of your painting after you left it to be influenced by the forces of nature. You might intuit that this means you need to pay closer attention to this health challenge. In looking at the nature painting as a whole, you might see that your fatigue requires your attention because it has displaced all the other health concerns that you want to attend to. You might decide that resting and not being so ambitious about fixing other health problems needs to be your priority right now.

Whatever you learn from working with your nature painting, be sure to apply the insights to your everyday life.

Bringing Nature's Healing Benefits Indoors

Many people, when asked to visualize something they find calming, will picture a nature scene, and typically one with water and blues and greens. In their mind's eye, they will experience a tranquil pond, a lake stretching out to meet the sky at the horizon, or an azure tropical lagoon. When you can't get outdoors into nature, you might want to experiment with using your imagination indoors to recreate the experience of nature. Close your eyes and envision a place in nature that you find restful. Or, look out a window at a scene of greenery and water, or even simply at a picture of a tranquil pond, while listening to a recording of natural sounds, and see how it affects your mood and sense of well-being.

A 2010 study published in the *International Journal of Environmental Research and Public Health* showed that natural sounds increase the speed of recovery from psychological stress.[12] Notice whether you feel calmer after a few minutes of listening to, say, the sound of a fountain, ocean waves, or a trickling creek. Is the effect, for you, similar to actually being outdoors? Try using recordings, photographs, videos, and even natural smells to make it easier to imagine being on a sunny beach or in a cool forest meditating next to a pond, when you are actually in an office with a window view of traffic, steel, and concrete. A shaman might say that the forest in your mind is as real as the one miles away. However, to actually be in nature would be ideal.

Some people choose to live in an area that is less developed so they can more easily experience nature. But even those who live in urban areas can receive nature's health benefits, as studies over the past 30 years have shown.[13] In a much-cited 1984 study, a researcher named Roger Ulrich and his team found that hospital surgery patients recover more quickly and even require fewer painkillers when their rooms for convalescing have views of nature.[14] Knowing this, you might choose to bring nature into your life through window views of trees or gardens.

Perhaps the underlying reason for this powerful effect is what happens to our brains when we are exposed to nature. We move from focused attention, which involves the frontal lobes and the sympathetic nervous system, to involuntary attention and a more diffuse focus, as a result of the parasympathetic nervous system having been activated. While there are stimuli in nature, we usually feel no need to deal with them because nothing calls to us "Watch out!" or "Over here!" The line of ants can continue along their path as a squirrel darts up a tree and leaves flutter in the wind. In response, we can simply be present instead of having to react to any of it.

Attention restoration theory says that this state of involuntary attention is relaxing. In a 2013 *Atlantic* magazine article called "How Nature Resets Our Minds and Bodies," Adam Alter wrote, "While man-made landscapes bombard us with stimulation, their natural counterparts give us the chance to think as much or as little as we'd like, and the opportunity to replenish exhausted mental resources."[15] I would say Carl Jung was referring to involuntary attention when he said that if we engage the unconscious and access an inner figure or a symbol, we should "contemplate it and carefully observe how the picture begins to unfold or to change. Don't try to make it into something, just do nothing but observe what its spontaneous changes are."[16] A Buddhist might say involuntary attention correlates with a state of "witnessing mind" or "observing mind," or perhaps "no mind."

If you can't be in nature, you might bring nature to you through houseplants. According to a study published in the journal *Horticultural Technology* in 2000, when plants and natural lighting or full-spectrum lighting were introduced to an office, a hospital x-ray lab, and a school-room, those who spent considerable time in these spaces experienced less fatigue as well as fewer headaches and dry throats. [17] We do know that plants remove certain chemicals from the air—chemicals that may be present in modern buildings—which may explain the results of the study.

I encourage you to try using the practices and exercises in this book when you are by a lake, on a beach, in the woods, or even in a backyard or a garden. Journal while you are sitting in the sun. Notice how it feels to use the practices and exercises, such as the ones for discovering your current health story, when you are outdoors in a natural area as opposed to indoors. If you use any of them indoors, you might want to try using natural objects, essential oils, and sounds to engage your senses, or do them in front of a window with a view of nature. Pay attention to whether bringing nature into the room in some way makes it easier for you to access your unconscious, or if your experience of the exercises is enhanced. For example, what does it feel like to do a dialogue while bathed in natural sunlight streaming through windows that provide a view of a grassy hill or a garden?

You might also experiment with doing the exercises while playing recordings of nature sounds, with or without soothing music, or recordings of shamanic drumming or rattling, to complement these sounds and help you transition from an ordinary state of consciousness to a trancelike state in which you have greater access to your unconscious.

Also, the exercises in Chapter Seven: Working with the Healing Elements of Nature involve the four traditional elements of nature: fire, earth, water, and air. Listen to your intuition about how to interact with these elements and to discover what they mean for you. You may work with them outdoors, of course—or you can work indoors, using natural objects such as sticks, shells, stones, or a feather.

Other natural energies you can work with include the energies of the sun, the moon, the night and the day, the sky, the earth—and any natural area such as a lake, river, forest, mountain, or desert. When you work with any of these energies, pay attention to your breathing so you can more easily calm the busy activity of your rational mind and awaken your unconscious mind. Consider opening sacred space, cleansing your energy field, and doing mindful breathing before doing an exercise in nature—and if you open sacred space, be sure to close it.

Intuition, Bliss, and Interconnectedness in Nature

Working in nature, having all your senses awakened as you spend time in your natural home, and observing and experiencing the rhythms of nature, may play a role in something many people have observed: that nature seems to enhance your intuition and, therefore, your ability to access your inner knowing.

Many people find it easier to observe what is typically hidden from the conscious, rational mind when they are outdoors in a natural setting. Perhaps being in nature facilitates being in touch with your inner wisdom because you are more tuned in to your own natural rhythms and yourself and your body as part of a natural world where things change and age. Noticing how trees that have been struck by lightning grow new branches might help you see that you, too, can find new ways to grow after an illness or injury. It might help you realize you can experience wellness without trying to revive what is old and can no longer be brought back to life. Nature is ever adapting and transforming, which teaches us about our own ability to change our experiences and thus our stories.

You might observe animals eating, and notice whether nature gives you messages about your own eating habits. You might consciously choose to become aware of your body's movements, strength, balance, flexibility, and stamina as you hike, swim, or climb in nature. Perhaps the movements of certain animals remind you of how your body moves. In yoga and in Chinese Shaolin kung fu, some poses are named after animals. Presumably, these poses were inspired by ancient people observing the movements of creatures and hoping to learn from embodying them. Ponder whether you are able to quickly and adroitly respond to danger, moving away from it, like a chipmunk darting. Or do you ignore your instincts and remain in physically and emotionally unhealthy situations, like an opossum?

To adapt to the rhythms and customs of society, we have learned to ignore what our bodies and instincts tell us to do. The movements of creatures in nature can remind you of how you, too, may be following the edicts of your rational mind, and beliefs and ideas you internalized long ago, to the detriment of your body. You may have learned to push yourself when you are sick, using medications to mask symptoms, rather than rest. You might observe an unusual spot for an animal's nest and realize you have been pressuring yourself to create a nest of safety in one place and not considering all your options. The stress of trying to figure out what you need to do in order to experience wellness can blind you to the lessons nature teaches every day.

You can spend time in nature with the intention of learning more about your sexuality, your body image, your experiences of hormonal changes in middle age—and any symptoms or acute ailments you have. Perhaps the plants, sky, ground, or water can teach you something about flexibility or balance.

A participant in one of my workshops said she had done some mountain biking and, when riding downhill, observed that it is harder to steer when applying the brakes. She said, "I realized that sometimes we must let go and trust the process rather than applying brakes and being cautious." An insight such as this could be an important realization if you are frustrated with a treatment you are undergoing that is causing you to have plateaus and setbacks you find demoralizing.

Perhaps we become more intuitive in nature because we cease being highly distracted by the stimulation in an artificial environment. When we are indoors, away from nature, we are regularly exposed to unexpected, stressful stimulation. This can include upsetting news or visual images that greet us when we turn on a television or mobile device, along with information we feel the need to process and make sense of right away. The habit of allowing ourselves to be constantly stimulated changes the brain over time, making it hard to quiet its constant activity. The frontal cortex (involved in thinking and deciding) and amygdala (involved in fear and anger) can become chronically overactive, leading to brooding and constant internal chatter rather than a sense of oneness and tranquility. In fact, according to a Stanford University study, walking in nature, compared to walking along a busy highway, quiets the part of the brain involved in rumination and brooding—the subgenual prefrontal cortex.[18]

When you are in a natural environment (and, possibly, when you trick your brain into believing you are there), the activity in your limbic brain and your prefrontal cortex quiets down and the integration between these areas is increased, as explained earlier. To be more specific, as your nervous system enters a parasympathetic state, you begin to experience alpha and theta brain waves, which are slower than the beta brain waves you experience in ordinary consciousness. Ruminative self-talk that can quickly turn negative is reduced. Your sense of time may shift, and you might feel light, warm, and energized as well as joyful and contented—just as you might during the trancelike state achieved as part of shamanic journeying. While in this state, your emotional center may still be active, but you are able to integrate its experiences better because the logical, thinking part of your brain (the frontal cortex) is communicating with your emotional center in the limbic brain. Anger and worry are put into perspective.[19]

Additionally, in an integrated brain state, you are able to access from your unconscious information that your conscious mind avoided processing. You might discover that the emotions and thoughts that come to the surface are not so frightening after all and you can handle facing them. You can integrate your conscious and unconscious thoughts and emotions more easily. Your memories can live within you differently, and you find you can remember past traumas in ways that benefit you and foster wisdom. Stories of victimhood and suffering can give way to stories of triumph and survival because of the new perceptions you have as a result of integrating the forebrain and the limbic, emotional brain.

Learning about Yourself from Nature

Regardless of which techniques you use to alter your consciousness, or whether it simply shifts as you spend time in nature, you can learn much from observing and being fully present with the natural world around you. The more you experience yourself in a natural environment, the more you may come to develop wisdom about your life, your health, and your experience of your body. You learn from the creation, movement, and melting of glaciers, the rise and fall and extinction of species, the ravages of nature and its ways of restoration. You can learn from the movement of water as it changes from cloud to rain, from ice to water. Watch the currents of a river or stream, or sit at the intersection between a river and a bay, and contemplate how these transformations relate to your own life.

Reflect on your body's changes over the years, and how it adapts, moves, and expresses resilience through illness and recovery. Think about how your body feels when the weather is windy versus when the air is still, or when the humidity is high versus when it drops and the air becomes crisp. What can these experiences tell you about your body and its relationship with nature? How does your body, and its systems, reflect nature?

Are there times of the year when your health story is more satisfying? If so, why? When does your health story become less satisfying? Do you have seasonal affective disorder (SAD) when the amount of sunlight is minimal? If so, how might you counteract the depressive effects of low natural light? If you sleep more in the winter when daylight is less intense and lasts for a much shorter time, is that a problem for you? Or is there a way to take advantage of how nature cues you to sleep more—or less—and thus foster better health?

If there are natural places or climates where you feel healthier, happier, and more vitalized, try to spend more time there. Find ways to get past any obstacles that prevent you from reconnecting with nature and Source.

Nature is a great teacher, modeling the balance and harmony we seek to experience in our bodies and in our environments. As you observe nature, and interact with it respectfully, you can begin to feel connected to something larger than yourself that supports you in experiencing health and wellness. You may better recognize your harmful impact on nature and end up changing your behavior to be more respectful of it.

When you are out in nature, take time to thank it for working with you. Give back as best you can. Tread softly on the earth, doing your best not to damage it through your presence—for example, take note of bluffs that are eroding, and do not walk on them.

Then, too, you might make small changes to your lifestyle that contribute to the health of your body and to the health of the planet; the health of both are intertwined. Ingesting highly processed foods and man-made chemicals confuses your body and the earth, which receives them when they leave your body and go into the environment through your body's waste products (for example, sweat or breath).

Help keep waters on the earth clean, and reduce your use of plastics. Recycle what you can. Remember to bring your reusable bags to the store so you do not end up with extra plastic bags. Buy products with minimal packaging, much of which is plastic. Plastics break down into small pieces that get into waterways and into fish, which are eaten by larger fish, which we eat for our health. You are eating the plastics you throw away without thinking, so help keep the earth clean and unpolluted and the air clean and unpolluted.

As you are able to realize, conceptualize, and visualize your health as part of a larger web of life, you will increasingly seek out healthy experiences and make healthier choices. In the next chapter, you will learn to work with the specific energies related to the four elements on the planet that indigenous people have recognized as having healing energies: earth, water, air, and fire. These elements can be encountered and worked with as archetypal energies with particular qualities.

CHAPTER SEVEN

Working with the Healing Elements of Nature

From a shamanic standpoint, when we work with nature and the earth, our natural home, we interact with energies associated with the land, air, sky, and water as well as the stones, rivers, clouds, animals, and plants. Natural energies may be seen as archetypal, that is, as having qualities that one might associate with themes. In indigenous traditions, the energy of the sun, a fire, a river, and other features of the natural world were perceived as having characteristics beyond what a scientist would describe as emanating from these natural phenomena. To a shaman or a Jungian, the moon might represent the mother, or feminine power. Rivers and lakes have traditionally been associated with goddesses, fertility, abundance, giving birth—or rebirth.

Your own experiences of the elements might make you aware of different archetypal energies associated with them. As you work with the rituals in this chapter, all of which involve engagement with natural elements, be open to your own, unique understanding of their messages for you. There is no right or wrong way to interpret the movement of the waves of a lake as you sit quietly with them and open to their energy. A campfire has more than one way of expressing its energy to you: as flames, embers, and sparks. What you make of the smoke, the crackle, and the transformation of wood to coals and ash may be quite different from what someone else interprets when observing these natural phenomena.

Core Elements in Nature

For the purposes of healing, I encourage you to work with four natural elements: earth, water, air, and fire. They are all manifestations of Source's energy. These elements are commonly found in Native American traditions as well as European traditions. The latter gave birth to the tarot and its four suits, namely, pentacles (earth), cups (water), swords (air), and wands (fire). The European four-element tradition may have been rooted in the ancient Greek philosophers' belief that the natural world is composed of these four elements and complemented by a fifth one, ether, that transcended the limitations of the material world.

In Hinduism, we find the same five elements, whereas in Buddhism we find the four without ether. Chinese tradition identifies the key elements of the material world as earth, metal, water, fire, and wood. One might consider wood and metal to be associated with the earth since they are products of it. You might want to work with Ayurvedic medicine associations, which involve elements working together and affecting various bodily systems. I work with four elements—earth, water, air, and fire—but you should feel free to draw on any tradition you like in your healing work.

Some believe each of the elements has specific qualities. Theosophist writer Alice Bailey, in her book *A Treatise on White Magic,* explains that earth has effects on our physical bodies, water on our emotional bodies, and air on our spiritual bodies. Over the years, in doing healing work and reading about various wisdom traditions and belief systems, I have come across many possible interpretations of the qualities of the four elements, including:

- **Earth:** physicality, stability, manifestation, a quality of being grounded and in touch with everyday activities, taking action rather than simply having an idea or an emotional desire to do something, Mother Earth
- **Water:** the unconscious (from Jungian tradition), blood, passion,[1] the emotions, feeling rather than thinking or doing, going with the flow, flexibility, fluidity, cleansing or purifying
- **Air:** mental energy, ideas, creativity, wisdom, freedom, intelligence
- **Fire:** passion or drive, courage, enthusiasm, destructiveness, transformation, a call to change, conflict between people or within a person, light energy

To bring to life a new health story, you might work with these four elements to discover how you relate to the archetypal energies traditionally associated with them. You might find you need more earth energy to ground yourself in practices supportive of better health outcomes, or you might need to work with the energy of water to cleanse yourself of anxiety or fear that is affecting your body and bring in new energies that help you feel confident and hopeful.

I encourage you to engage the energies of earth, water, air, and fire to get rid of things that don't serve you and bring in things that do. All of the elements have a quality of movement or transformation. Fire turns wood into smoke and flame and ash; air and water move things from here to there, often altering the objects they move or exert force upon (canyons carved by rivers, for example). Even the earth can transform things, turning seeds into plants.

The elements work with and contain aspects of each other, because all are intertwined within nature. You should feel free to open yourself to the archetypal energy of any element that seems to call to you when you are outdoors. However, if you deliberately and ritualistically work with one element at a time, it might help you to engage its archetypal energy, learn from it, and work with it differently.

Your Relationships with the Elements

Again, as you interact with representations of the archetypal energies associated with these elements, you may find you have unexpected, personal relationships with the energies. For you, water may not feel soothing and reassuring; it might feel overwhelming, or out of your control, like rushing floodwaters. If you nearly drowned as a child, water could have an ominous quality for you that you might want to explore. If you enjoyed swimming and playing in the water as a child, water might have a quality of renewal and rejuvenation for you.

Pay attention to the forms elements take as you encounter them, and work with them. Because water takes many forms, when you work with it during a journey to bring something out and something else in, you might encounter it as flowing, or as an iceberg that refuses to budge. You might experience it as still and deep, in the form of a pond or lagoon, or as mist or clouds. By dialoguing with water in whatever form it appears, you may be able to change your relationship with it so you can reclaim your ability to "go with the flow." You might gain the ability to patiently abide the slow process of transformation, which is reflected in the melting of ice or the evaporation of water droplets.

As you begin to work with the natural elements, notice that each of them is not only around you but within you. You have air inside you—not just in your lungs but in your bloodstream, as oxygen. Your body is mostly made up of water, and humans, like all land animals, evolved from life forms that first arose in the sea.

We carry that lineage within us. Although you don't have literal fire within you, the chemical and electrical reactions in your body are one way in which "fire" exists within it. Minerals found in the earth and in the human body could be thought of as the earth element within you.

The energies of the four elements can be out of balance in your body (an idea found in Ayurvedic medicine). You can have too much water and have edema or too little and be dehydrated. You can have too little air, for example, if you have insufficient oxygen (although only about one-fifth of the air we breathe is actually oxygen).

You might have too much air: an overdose of pure oxygen from breathing using an oxygen tank could damage your body, although most of us will probably experience "too much air" as gas and bloating.

"Too much earth" in Ayurvedic medicine would mean loose bowels (the body trying to eliminate excess solid waste) while too little would mean constipation (holding on to waste). "Too much earth" for you might also mean a blockage or tumor, because there is a solid mass where there should be a flow of energy and fluids, while "too little earth" might mean inability of the blood to clot and the slow healing of wounds (commonly associated with diabetes).

As for fire, you might experience inflammation, which can be thought of as "fire." You may need inflammation to fight a pathogen, but once the invasive bacteria or foreign object is gone, the inflammation needs to be reduced. At that point, you have "too much fire." A fever might be a manifestation of "too much fire." According to Traditional Chinese Medicine (TCM), having the chills or circulatory problems might be thought of as having "too little fire."

Whether or not you subscribe to any of these systems of understanding our relationship to our bodies and the natural world, knowing some of the associations may help you as you write a new story of your health. Because our bodies are so closely related to nature, the home we evolved to experience, exploring what an imbalance of earth, air, fire, or water might mean to you might yield valuable insights and help you access healing energies associated with the elements.

Ideas for Elemental Healing

Although in their physical forms the elements of earth, water, air, and fire can be contaminated, their energetic essence is pure. Working with them energetically, you can use them for cleansing, purifying, fortifying, taking in, getting rid of, and balancing your body and its systems as well as your energy body.

When you engage one of the elements energetically, you can ask it to give you whatever it is you need. For example, water might give you an infusion of its energy, a cleansing/releasing, or both. Use your intuition to guide you in how you could work with actual water to bring in the energy you need and release the energy you would like to release. Similarly, with fire, you can ask it if you need more or less of its energy and then work with fire ritualistically to ensure your energy changes.

Let the elements guide you as to how you should work with them. Your intuition and the spirit of the element can be trusted to take out, to give, and to balance what you need. For example, if you are drawn to work with plants and rocks—aspects of the element earth—you might ask particular plants or rocks what they are willing to give to you, what they are willing to take from you, and what kind of balancing you might experience as a result of working with them.

As you ponder an element's symbolic meaning, allow your intuition to influence your perception and understanding. What are the qualities of this element found in nature? How do you experience its archetypal energy as a force in your health story? Is there too much fire in your body, or do you need to burn away something in order to experience less pain associated with your medical condition?

Experiment and learn to trust your experiences as you work with the elements. Set aside what you believe you know about the qualities of earth, water, air, and fire, and listen imaginatively whenever you interact with them as energies. When you are finished working with an element, thank it for helping you.

You might also use a ritual to solidify your intention to follow through on any changes in your health story you committed to while working with the elements. For example, you might plant a seed, or replant a seedling or small plant, water it, and use the plant as a reminder of your vow to write and bring to life a new health story.

Depending on your spiritual beliefs, you might recognize nature as

Source, or as a living manifestation of Source's creative energy and intention. As you work with nature, be open to your experiences and new insights about the relationship between your consciousness and that of Source, as well as your relationship to nature and its wisdom and healing energies.

Working with Nature in Particular Places

To work with the elements of nature, you can be indoors, using natural items ritualistically—perhaps a bundle of burning sage (known as a "smudging stick") or a feather to represent air, a rock to represent earth, a dish of water or a shell to represent the water in nature, or other objects that evoke these elements for you. You could use a candle to represent fire. However, it can be much more powerful to work with nature in an area outdoors, away from urban noise and lights, fully immersed in the sensory and energetic experience of a natural setting.

Choose a place where you sense you will be able to balance the energies affecting you, letting go of energies you have in excess and drawing in others you need. Once I was at the house of a shaman in Peru. While waiting for him, I walked around his yard and lay down under a tree. It seemed right and good to lie in that specific place, and I felt both at peace and invigorated. When the shaman returned, he smiled as he approached me and said that where I chose to rest was a particularly powerful healing spot that others who had visited him had been drawn to.

You might choose to let the earth herself suggest to you where to stop and work with her. Then, too, you might want to do rituals or use expanded-awareness practices in natural places identified as having healing qualities. The earth has many energy vortexes, spots where healing is easier to achieve because the earth's energy is available to you. Like a chakra, a vortex of energy is funnel shaped. It is the most narrow at the earth, where it pulls up energy that spirals upward to the broad top. These "earth chakras" can be found in Mt. Fuji, Japan; Glastonbury and Shaftesbury, England; Lake Titicaca, Peru; Sedona, Arizona; and elsewhere. In Sedona, the vortexes are said to have specific healing energies: Some bring in what your body needs to heal, others release what your body needs to let go of, and others balance your energies by doing both. The experience of doing healing work in these natural energy vortexes can be very powerful.

Tara, a participant in one of my workshops, talked about how she had harshly judged her body, resentful of its limitations. A trip to the mountainside of Assisi, Italy, associated with St. Francis, allowed her to feel more compassion for her body as she experienced a sense of connection to this Catholic saint. She said she returned with less tiredness, feeling revivified by the experience. I believe there is a special energy in places such as this, and that these spots actually have a consciousness you can engage and dialogue with.

If you can't or do not wish to travel to a place designated as having a particular energy associated with healing, you can simply reconnect with nearby spots in nature you feel you are drawn to—as I did at my shaman friend's home. In the following exercise, you will locate a specific place outdoors where you can work with nature and its healing elements.

Arrange to spend an hour or more in a natural area where you can work uninterrupted—a backyard, perhaps, or a park. You might choose a place where you played as a child, or which holds positive memories for you. It might be a place you are drawn to because of its energetic qualities. You could choose to open sacred space, cleanse your energy field, and do mindful breathing before you begin or you can simply allow nature to draw you into a state of expanded-awareness as you breathe mindfully.

EXPANDED-AWARENESS PRACTICE: CONNECT WITH A
HEALING SPACE IN NATURE

As you come to the natural area, breathe mindfully and reduce the activity of your mind as you tune in to the present moment. Notice the sensation of your inhalation and exhalation. Observe how you feel in your body as you stand on the ground. Observe the sensations of the sun on your skin and the uneven surface of the earth beneath your feet. Notice the natural sounds of birds, leaves fluttering in the wind, or insects buzzing.

Take several minutes to simply remain present in nature, attuned to your body, your surroundings, and the natural connection between your body and your surroundings.

As you sense your unity with nature, form a silent question about your health, asking this natural area what needs to be taken away for you to achieve a particular health outcome and bring to life a new and better story of your health.

Then, notice whether you feel drawn to a specific place that can help you take away what you need to release, such as a patch of grass or a spot underneath a particular tree.

If you do feel drawn to a specific place, walk to it. Stand, sit, or lie down in this location—whatever you sense you should do. Focus on the present moment and any sensations of energy being released from your body.

Observe those sensations, without trying to analyze where they are coming from or what energy is being released. Let your intuition guide you in understanding what you are letting go of and returning to nature to be recycled.

When you feel you have released energy you no longer need, thank this space for helping you.

Now, formulate a new question, asking what needs to be brought in for you to achieve a particular health outcome and bring to life a new story of your health. Remain focused on the sensations you are experiencing in the present moment, simply noticing them. Notice whether you feel you should move.

Follow your intuition's guidance. Whether you remain where you are or move to a space you sense will bring you the energy you need, observe what it feels like to be connecting to the healing energy of nature. Remain present with it until you feel you have received what you need to receive.

Ask this natural area, which has healing energy, whether it has a message for you about your health, and listen to the answer. Dialogue with this place if you like, asking it what insights it has for you.

When you are ready to leave, touch the earth with your bare hands and thank this natural area for working with and guiding you.

After using this expanded-awareness practice, close sacred space (if you opened it) and, later, journal about your experiences.

A woman named Ruth chose to dialogue with the ocean and beach near her home to learn more about her health story and get help in bringing it to life. She was in perimenopause and wanted to overcome some of its more troublesome symptoms: insomnia, weight gain in the belly, and hot flashes. Ruth had the following dialogue.

RUTH: I am transitioning into menopause. What message do you have for me about this transition?

OCEAN: Where my water meets the shore it is blurred and soft. There is no straight line. Water and sand meet in softness, always moving and changing their relationship to each other. Be soft, not hard, during this transition. Flow. Connect with my ebb and flow.

RUTH: I understand my "flow" is unpredictable so I don't know when it's coming or even if it's coming back. I hear you saying I should be soft, but I want to know what to do about the insomnia I have developed, and the hot flashes, and the weight I've gained in my belly. I hate how I look. I don't like these changes, and I want my body to return to what it was before.

OCEAN: You won't find the perfection and control you seek. You are changing. Stop trying so hard to control this transition and how you experience it. You can't hold back the tide. The flow happens as it is meant to happen. You are trying too hard to fix your body and get it to conform to your idea of what it should be like at this time. Your hormones are flowing as they want to flow. You can't control them. They come and go, like the hot flashes. Your insomnia comes and goes. Be present with it. Be accepting. Look at how smooth the strip of sand on the beach is right now. It's perfect, but the wind will blow, the tide will come in, and the new arrangement will be perfect, too. This moment has perfection in it, but you're blind to it because you want everything perfect and controlled—you want to go back to what you thought was perfect. Pay attention to the perfection of your body now. It is doing what it needs to do.

RUTH: How can I let go of my need to control my body? How can I see my body's perfection as it is?

OCEAN: Be fully present when you eat. Pay attention and eat slowly. Pay attention when you move. Notice your body's need to move and get up and move right then. Don't wait for the perfect time to get the perfect amount of the perfect exercise. Be present with your insomnia. Be grateful for your changing body. Say a prayer of gratitude for your perfect body in this moment. Be open to what you are becoming. Feel curiosity. Open to it, and let sleep come when sleep comes. Don't try to force it.

RUTH: How do I let go of the anxiety about wasting time when I am awake in the middle of the night? Can you take that away from me?

OCEAN: Change your relationship to time. Perspective. You are in transition and need to be present in it. You are not supposed to rush forward to some sort of goal and "conquer" your body or your insomnia. Do not measure the hours of sleep you got. Stop looking at clocks and thinking about numbers. This is your time to get in touch with your body's needs and your spirit's needs.

RUTH: Is there anything I can do for you?

OCEAN: Be present with me. Spend time with me. Make time for me so I can change your perspective and your relationship to time. You will eat better in time. You will sleep better in time. First you have to release your fear of time. Release it to me.

RUTH: Thank you. I will make time for being with you. I think in doing so, I'm making time for being with me, for honoring myself and my relationship to you.

OCEAN: I'm always here for you, with you, but you forget! Stop thinking and fixing so much. Just sit with me. Just be.

You might not get answers to all your questions in one dialogue, and as I said earlier, you might have to dialogue again to get answers. You might not know all the questions you want to ask until you engage nature and her healing elements. Encounter the elements in different ways, and you might gain different insights or experience their energy differently.

Working with the Element of Earth

In natural spaces, the ground we walk on—the earth element—takes different forms. The ground itself may be bare dirt, sand, or rock, or it may be covered with grass, sticks, and dead leaves. When you walk on the ground in your bare feet, you may or may not be able to see what you are about to step on. How comfortable would you feel walking on the earth when you can't see what you might be stepping on with your bare feet? Do you trust the earth to be solid beneath your feet? Do you need to pay closer attention to your relationship with the earth as you move forward one step at a time?

You might experiment with different ways of walking on the earth and let your intuition guide you in understanding what the experience is about for you and how it relates to your health. When walking in nature, your feet and your leg muscles have to adjust to the uneven surfaces, inclines, and slippery spots. Try walking with focused attention and noticing what you can learn about your balance and your relationship to the earth's uneven surface. What does walking on uneven ground tell you, if anything, about the chapter in your story on movement, balance, strength, stamina, and exercise? What can the earth teach you about strength and perseverance, or movement and rest? The earth is the most solid of the elements and might have lessons for you about movement versus remaining in one place, about not forcing issues or avoiding or running away from them.

We rarely lie on the ground, except perhaps at the beach, perhaps when on vacation. Yet doing so can bring us in touch with our relationship to the earth and help us to feel the earth's energy and its connection to our own energy field. Use the following expanded-awareness exercise to get in touch with the earth. You might try doing it when lightly dressed to see how it feels for you to have a lot of skin-to-earth contact and then try it again when fully clothed, perhaps even when there is snow on the ground or it is muddy or wet. If you have physical discomfort when lying on hard ground, you might lie on a mat with parts of your arms and legs touching the earth itself. Lying on the ground can make you more aware of your body and your skin, as you feel tactile sensations and adjust to the uneven surface you are lying upon.

To do this exercise, find a place where you will be uninterrupted and safe as you lie on the ground. You might open sacred space, cleanse your energy field, and do mindful breathing, quieting your mind.

EXPANDED-AWARENESS PRACTICE: LYING ON THE EARTH

Lower yourself to the ground, and continue to do mindful breathing. Notice whether your breathing changes as you lie there. Notice the sensations under your skin and under your body. Notice whether you feel vulnerable or safe. Observe any emotions or sensations that come up for you.

Now, ask the earth, "What message do you have for me about my health?"

Dialogue with it, asking what you can release, or give to it, and asking what it can give you.

Let the dialogue flow naturally, suggesting questions to you.
When you are finished, thank the earth for helping you.
Slowly, return to ordinary consciousness.

Close sacred space (if you opened it), and journal about your experience.

Earth is like a mother because she brings forth life and nurtures it. She grows plants that clean the air and transform sunlight into food—not only for the plants but for other forms of life in the food chain. What could the earth nurture in you? Could she transform something for you by allowing you to grow something different, helping you to let die that which you no longer need?

The earth has energy that might revitalize you, even as you release into it something that needs to be discharged from your energy field and body that can then be recycled. What will you give to the earth? What can you unburden yourself of, releasing it to the loving Mother Earth? What can she give to you?

As you spend time outdoors, connect to the earth so you can learn how it can help you let go of what you don't need and bring in what will benefit you. Pay attention to the qualities of the earth that remind you of some aspect of your health. Journal about what the V-shaped flock of flying geese can tell you about managing your pain, or about what an eroding bluff can teach you about how you are relating to your body's weaknesses and changes due to the passage of time.

Indoors, it can be difficult to feel a connection to the earth, learn from it, and engage it energetically. Having plants, rocks, crystals, sticks, driftwood, acorns, or leaves in your home or office is one way to feel you are in touch with the earth. You can look at them or touch them when you want to feel grounded. When you meditate, experiment with how it feels to have these small elements of earth near you, clutched in your hand or resting on your body as you lie on the floor. You might also want to dialogue with them, honoring them as representations of the earth and her ability to heal and nurture you.

Again, consider going into a natural area outdoors to work with a particular place on earth that can help you write and bring to life a new health story—whether that means you trek to Machu Picchu in Peru, visit the Black Hills of South Dakota, return to the park by your childhood home, or simply let yourself be drawn to a spot in a nature preserve.

Working with the Element of Water

We can experience water as clouds and rain, as well as steam, mist, dew, ice, sleet, snow, and hail. Water can be contained within a lake or pond or surround us as fog or snowflakes dancing in the wind. We can commune with water outside, by a body of water such as a river or ocean, or indoors, as we sit by an indoor fountain, swim in a pool, or take a bath or shower.

Often, we encounter water as moving. What might it take away from you as you shower or let yourself float down a stream while sitting in an inner tube? What might it bring into you as you soak in a tub or swim in a pool or natural body of water?

When you swim, you have to balance your movements if you want to swim in a straight line. If you are a swimmer, pay attention the next time you enjoy this activity. Try to swim in a straight line with your eyes closed. Can paying attention to balancing your movements help you swim straight? As you swim, open yourself to what you can learn about your health. Are there lessons about movement, flexibility, stamina, strength, and exercise? What do you need to push away, slowly and methodically? What can being in the water tell you about your breathing, your lungs, and your heart?

Working with water can also teach you about cleansing toxins as part of achieving balance and good health. Water can be purified through the distillation process, and the toxic residue can then be discarded. You, too, carry various toxins in your fluid systems. How can you become purified? What needs to be carried out of your system, and what needs to be brought in and distributed throughout your body by your blood and other fluids? You might want to work at being more aware of the purity of what you take in and your body's ability to filter toxins. Do you need to drink more water?

Do you need to take in more of something to help you detoxify your body and energy system? You might visualize your kidneys and liver cleansing your blood. Do you have difficulty with elimination, suggesting that you need to be able to flush out toxins better with the help of water? Are there emotional toxins you need to release through crying, swimming, bathing, showering, or offering up your grief, anger, or fear to a body of water that can carry it away or dilute it and recycle it?

Simply being near water can remind you of your close relationship with it. Our bodies are composed mostly of water, and humans began as one-celled creatures swimming in the oceans.

Water has traditionally been used in ceremonies to mark birth—baptisms and christenings, for example. It can bring in something new and cleanse us, washing away the old. As we shed skin cells and dirt on our bodies, we can feel renewed. What emotions might you bring in or release by working ritually with water? You might dialogue with water to find out what it can take away and bring in so that you can live according to a new health story.

The following expanded-awareness exercise can be used to replenish and energetically detoxify yourself with water. Prepare for this exercise by going to a river, stream, lake, pond, or ocean. If you can't find a place outside in nature to do this exercise, do it in a bathtub or shower.

You might start this practice by opening sacred space, cleansing your energy field, and doing mindful breathing. Immerse yourself in the water, if it is safe to do so; otherwise, immerse yourself partially. (For example, if you are working with a body of water outdoors and are not a strong swimmer, you can stand at the water's edge or simply dangle your bare feet and legs in it as you sit on a pier.)

EXPANDED-AWARENESS PRACTICE: RELEASING, REPLENISHING, AND BALANCING WITH WATER

As you feel the water against your skin, notice how it feels: the temperature, the fluidity, and any other qualities it has.

Ask the water, "What message do you have for me about my health?" Wait for the answer to be revealed to you. Remain present and patient.

When you are ready, ask, "What can you take away from me to help me experience better health?" Again, wait patiently for the answer.

Imagine the water drawing out of your body and energy field what is no longer serving you—something that may be toxic or something you simply no longer need. Let the water wash it away.

Now, ask, "What can you bring me?"

Imagine your skin soaking in the water and drawing in whatever will replenish you and help you bring to life a new health story. Observe what it is offering you, and how it feels to receive that.

When you feel replenished and balanced, ask the water if it has any other messages for you. When you feel you have learned what you need to learn, and made the exchange of energy you needed, thank the water for helping you.

Close sacred space (if you opened it), and ponder what you experienced and journal about it. If you received any insights that would be helpful, apply them to your life.

Working with the Element of Air

Air, with its component of oxygen, is essential for human life. Air is all around you: still, turbulent, humid, damp, dry, hot, and cold. In your imagination, and also outside in nature, you can learn to seek out the qualities of air that you need. When do you need to experience the air as very still? When do you need to be in a brisk wind or a gentle breeze?

We feel air but don't see it unless it is moving something—dandelion seeds, smoke, morning fog that rolls away, clouds in the sky, or leaves that flutter on their branches or skip along a sidewalk in response to this elemental energy. When you see the air moving something, you might stop to ask, "When it comes to my health, what is moving that I am not seeing? What is changing that I am unaware of? Are there signs of movement or change that I have been overlooking?"

A common way to work with the element of air to bring about healing is to use sage to cleanse your energy field. Another way of engaging it is to wave a feather or shake a rattle, which moves the air as you cleanse your energy field.

The following exercise is a way of working with air to gain insights as well as draw in and release energies. It is best done on a windy day. If you like, open sacred space, cleanse your energy field, and do mindful breathing before using this practice.

EXPANDED-AWARENESS PRACTICE: HEALING WITH THE ELEMENT OF AIR

On a windy day, go outside and set the intention to open yourself to any messages and energies that air might bring you.

Notice the movement of objects around you as they are blown by the wind. Observe how it feels to have the wind blowing your hair and pressing against your skin before settling down again.

Ask the wind, "What message do you have for me about my health story?" (Alternatively, you can ask it about a specific health challenge of yours.)

Wait for the answer. Then, ask the wind, "What can you take away from me that I need to release in order to live according to a new health story?" Wait for the answer.

Then, each time you exhale, imagine that you are releasing something you no longer need. You might say to yourself silently, "Release" or "Out" or "No more" with each exhalation.

When you feel you have done the releasing you need to do, ask the wind, "What can you bring me?" Open to receive whatever gift the wind has for you. Breathe in, and as you draw in air, you might say to yourself silently, "In" or "New" or whatever word feels natural to you.

Continue this exchange, inhaling what you need, exhaling what you do not need.

When you feel replenished energetically, thank the wind for working with you.

Close sacred space if you opened it. Journal about your experience.

Working with the Element of Fire

Fire provides heat, warmth, and comfort. It alters our food and transforms wood into smoke, ash, and flame. A fire contains embers that are dying down and burning out, and sparks that appear suddenly and can fly out from what is being burned, causing something else to catch on fire. It's difficult to contain fire, or control it—unless you deprive it of the element of air or you stop fueling it. Is there something in your health story that you need to stop fueling? Is there something that is out of control? Is there something you are trying too hard to contain that you need to let loose so transformation can occur?

Fire, whether it's on the beach, in a firepit, or emanating from a candle's wick, exerts a hypnotic influence on people around it and observing it. From our earliest days on the earth, we have gathered around fire and respected its power. It can destroy and transform. As you relate to the energy of fire, you are reconnecting to the creative energy of the sun. You can transform what's no longer working in your health story and begin to create something new.

Figuratively speaking, fire in your body keeps your internal temperature around 98.6° F. Are you too hot or too cold much of the time? What does that mean for you? Hot flashes, having cold hands and feet, and running a temperature are all physical ailments Western medicine can treat. But consider whether these experiences have messages for you—about fire, passion, transformation, or something else.

Your body contains chemical and electrical phenomena that can generate heat and the qualities of fire. You can learn to relate to those aspects of fire for clearing, adding, and balancing yourself. When do you need to be ignited, and when do you need to reduce the intensity of the fire within you? When do your symptoms flare up, and when do they die down?

You can work with a campfire or firepit to do the following exercise, in which you burn away what you no longer need and transform it to something you can use to change your health story. Prepare for this practice by assembling three small piles of sticks you can burn during the ritual and placing them near where you will sit, which will be next to the fire source. Because this is a ritual, it's best to work with opening and closing sacred space, as well as the preparatory practices you learned earlier.

Start a fire in a firepit, where there is no danger of the fire spreading beyond where you are working with it. Be sure to have a large container of water nearby to fully extinguish the fire afterward, or cover it with a layer of dirt to put the fire out completely—every last ember. Alternatively, you can work indoors, with a candle and a bowl of water where you can drop the burning sticks—a bowl you can later empty outside, returning the water and remnants of sticks to the earth.

You might begin by opening sacred space, cleansing your energy field, doing mindful breathing, and gravitating naturally to a comfortable position near the fire, with the sticks and the water by your side.

EXPANDED-AWARENESS PRACTICE: TRANSFORMING
WITH FIRE

As you look into the fire, pick up a stick. Blow into it the energy of some-thing you need to release in order to bring to life a new story of your health. Let your intuition suggest what that something may be.

For example, it might be your frustration over the need to man-age your chronic fatigue, or it might be your identification with your fatigue. It might be the belief that you can't manage your condition and lead a full, enjoyable life. It might be a habit that tends to make your fatigue worse.

As you place the stick in the fire, affirm aloud what you are releas-ing. Watch the stick burn. As it transforms to ash and smoke, listen to what your intuition is telling you. Is there wisdom to be gained as you perform this ritual? Do you feel a release?

Continue blowing into each stick something you wish to release. Remem-ber to affirm aloud what you are letting go of as you feed the stick to the fire to be transformed.

When you are finished and have exhausted the pile of sticks that embody what you want to release or get rid of, breathe deeply. Watch the sticks you placed in the fire transform as they burn.

Now, you will identify things you wish to gain—energies you would like to bring into your new health story, or new habits you would like to establish. Pick up a stick from the second pile and blow into it the intention to gain something for your health story.

You might want to express your wish aloud before placing the stick, which now embodies your intention to receive this energy or help establishing a new habit, in the fire.

Again, blow an intention into one stick at a time, and consider affirming your intention aloud before adding the stick to the fire. You might form the intention to experience strength and stamina in your body and flexibility in your joints, for example. You can simply allow your intuition to guide you as you pick up each stick and you recognize what you want to intend and say.

When you have exhausted the second pile of sticks, look into the fire and imagine the smoke of transformation, which holds for you wisdom and energies you need to replenish and reinvigorate yourself.

You may wish to use your hands to draw in replenishing energies from the fire in front of you, making sweeping motions toward your body and then placing the energy in any area of your body where you sense you could most use it. Continue drawing into yourself these healing energies until you feel you no longer need to do so.

Now you are ready to work with your third pile of sticks. You will blow into each of these sticks a wish for healing the collective and then feed them to the fire, one by one.

You might wish for all people to get the health care they need, for the waters of the earth to be cleaner, or for those with anxiety and depression to find peace, comfort, and joy.

When you have exhausted the third pile of sticks, watch as the energy of your expressed intentions turns to ash and to smoke that rises upward, carrying the energy to where it needs to go.

Thank the fire for helping you, and when you are ready, extinguish any flames, along with the embers, by pouring water on them. Be open to any messages you intuit when doing so.

If you opened sacred space, close it. Later, journal about your experience.

Having worked with expanded-awareness practices and journaling to identify your story and write a new one, your task now is to begin applying what you have learned. I suggest you journal about your observations as you notice how your new story is coming into being.

Is it easier for you to break old habits, for example? Do you feel differently about what you are experiencing? Is your health improving? Are you feeling optimistic that it can continue to improve?

There will come a time when you will want to revise your health story, perhaps because you are having a different, less satisfying experience of your health than you wanted or anticipated. You might realize you want to further shape your health story and focus on some chapters more than others. You may be struggling to accept your health as it is, despite the work you are doing to change it, or you may wish to be even more ambitious in writing and bringing to life a new story of your health. In the next chapter, you will work with the themes of acceptance and resistance, as well as look at how to acknowledge fears or discomfort with aging, dire prognoses, and your beliefs and feelings about your mortality, so that you can revise your health story in a way that works for you.

CHAPTER EIGHT

Revising the Story
of Your Health

As time passes, your health story will change. Will it be a satisfying one? Can it be acceptable or even pleasing to you, even if the events within it are not what you would have hoped they would be?

Sometimes, an unforeseen accident fundamentally alters a person's health story. What has happened is undeniable, and it must be integrated into the story. Moreover, there is no way to avoid seeing your health story change as you age. Your cells, organs, and bones will deteriorate eventually, despite any efforts you make to prevent aging. The telomeres, structures on the ends of your chromosomes, will shorten, reducing the number of times your cells will reproduce, bringing you closer to the moment when your physical experiences in this world will end.

However, there is an aspect of your health story you always have control over: how you tell it. You can choose to look at any deterioration or losses as signs that you need to commit more firmly to reducing emotional stress and living more healthfully. You can always write a new and more pleasing health story, even if your health worsens. You might not experience what you hope to experience, but you have more power to affect your story than it may appear on the surface.

Aging happens, and injuries and accidents occur, and diseases strike people who seem to have no predisposition to have them. Even so, no matter what happens in your health story, you get to decide which losses and changes you can accept and which you want to continue to fight. You have many choices about what to focus on and how to revise your health story.

Healthy Attitude, Healthy Aging

When it comes to aging and the natural transformation of health stories, the news is not all bad. Recent research cited by the American Psychological Association shows that baby boomers report lower stress than younger generations (Generation X and the Millennials), and those who are even older, past age 75, report even less stress.[1]

A 2014 Gallup poll showed that compared to people under 65, people over 65 are more likely to report they have supportive relationships, good community connections, physical stamina, and a sense of financial security. A Pew Research survey showed that people ages 18 to 64 expect that, as they age, they will experience stressful situations such as trouble paying bills, being a burden on others, feeling lonely, being sexually inactive, and suffering from a serious illness. Yet people over 65 report they are less likely to be having these experiences than their younger counterparts would expect. For example, the poll showed that 57 percent of younger people think they will experience memory loss as they get older while only 25 percent of the older people surveyed were actually dealing with this issue.[2]

What's more, many older people say they are happier than ever, even though they have symptoms of aging or health challenges. They attribute this to having a greater sense of appreciation for the simple pleasures of life—tending a garden, enjoying a glass of wine or a slow walk, bonding with their dogs or cats, or watching children play. Their perspective on what matters may have caused them to write and live according to a story called, "Every day is a blessing" or "Life is always a fascinating adventure, and there is always something new to learn."

As individuals, we have considerable control over how much effort we put into managing our stress, which allows us to reduce its deleterious effects on our bodies. We can also use the wisdom that comes from many years of life experiences to look at our health differently, from the perspective of the larger story of our lives.

As a result, changes in our appearance, aches and pains, and limitations in balance and flexibility may become easier to accept. What we have lost can be viewed within the context of what we have gained: more comfort with who we are, better interpersonal skills, greater clarity about what we want to experience, expertise in areas of interest gleaned as a result of years of practice and study, pride in accomplishment, a deeper sense of connection to Spirit, and so on.

Accepting Conditions You Can't Change

When you focus more on your health and what you can do going forward to influence it positively, it can become easier to accept what you can't change. You might also find that working on other aspects of your story, such as your spirituality or your career or vocation, helps you to feel a greater sense of purpose, which puts into perspective any health challenges you may have.

As we grow older, many of us begin to experience the consequences of our bad habits, which may have begun years before. As part of a revised health story, you may have to accept and forgive yourself for choices you made in the past. You may have to let go of bad habits that seemed relatively benign before, because now you are seeing the price you are paying for them.

You may be able to stop and even reverse the changes, at least to some degree. For example, some of the skin damage caused by sun exposure can be repaired. Surgeries can replace overworked and deteriorated knees, hips, and shoulders, making a significant difference in your ability to be pain-free and more flexible and active. Bypass surgery can return arteries to a previous state of health and functionality. The challenge then becomes finding ways to break the old habits that led to your arteries becoming clogged or to your skin becoming damaged.

Some people have access to procedures and medications likely to improve their health but hesitate to take advantage of these interventions as a result of their feelings about growing older and showing signs of aging in their skin and bodies. For example, a man might think he is being vain in wanting to surgically address drooping eyelids, but this condition can begin to interfere with eyesight, so undergoing surgery may not be vain after all. A woman might feel foolish for wanting to look younger, and ambivalent about making changes in her appearance, but an exploration of hidden themes might reveal she has avoided the painful reality that ageism is affecting her. If you are embarrassed and ashamed about wanting to look younger, those feelings may be reduced if you more deeply explore why you are resistant to addressing the issue of body image.

Let's say you decide to dialogue with your resistance to wearing hearing aids to improve your hearing. You may have read that hearing loss can affect your ability to communicate and even is associated with increased risk of depression. Through expanded-awareness practices and journaling, you might discover you are resistant to checking out hearing aids because you do not want to look old or disabled. If you face your true feelings and beliefs, and work differently with the wisdom and energies in your unconscious, you might become more open to the possibility of wearing a hearing aid. You might realize the payoffs outweigh the drawbacks, and you might be willing to let go of some of your discomfort with the aging process.

Most people would probably say that when it comes to growing older, they would be willing to tolerate a few aches and pains or minor conditions that are limiting in some way if it meant they could continue to enjoy most, if not all, of the activities they value. Preparing for your health story to change, as it inevitably will, does not have to mean giving up on your desire for a positive experience of health in the future. It may simply mean being more realistic and acknowledging that there are influences on your health story that you can't control completely.

Lyle, a man who attended one of my workshops simply because he was interested in having a satisfying health story as he aged, told me that journeying, along with dialoguing with health issues, made it easier for him to start thinking about his health and longevity differently. Previously, he hadn't worried about his health, but facing the truth about what the future might hold helped him discuss his health concerns with his family. Together, they came to some decisions about what to do if Lyle were ever to become dependent on his family for care as he grew older.

Honesty about where you are with your health right now, and what your prognosis is, can be more valuable than you might suspect initially. For evidence, we can look at what happens when people with serious, life-threatening illnesses get palliative care or even hospice care. (Palliative care focuses on keeping a patient comfortable and not being attached to the outcome, while hospice care is similar but designed for people whose illnesses are terminal and who are not expected to live for more than six months.) Some research shows that entering palliative care or hospice care not only improves the quality of life but extends it.[3]

We do not know why this is. Perhaps greater attention to what we value, such as interactions with loved ones, contributes to health and longer lifespans when we are in palliative or hospice care. Perhaps preparing for the possibility of death helps us to write and bring into being a new and more satisfying health story, while denial of the seriousness of our condition and resistance to healing relationships and our own personal wounds contributes to our illness and deterioration.

I have seen people who have stage 4 cancer use expanded-awareness practices and journaling to write a new story of their health and develop a different relationship with their disease. They become less focused on finding a cure for their disease and completely overcoming it, and more concerned about taking care of unfinished business with loved ones, such as having important conversations they neglected to have before. In talking to those closest to them, they asked and expressed forgiveness and love.

I recall one man, William, who said the experience of looking at his life from a broader perspective helped him to accept where he was, what he had and hadn't accomplished, and the fact that he might not live much longer. He said that before he had become terminally ill, he did not seem to have had the capacity to look at his life in this way. William explained he felt better able to be loving when having difficult conversations with his family. He had started to write poetry to express the deeper feelings and insights he was now experiencing. William told me he felt that his cancer was still an adversary he wanted to beat, but also a catalyst that was helping him to live more fully and expressively, with less anger at his situation.

After a session with me, in which he seemed to have good stamina and a positive energy, he announced he was going to take a long walk by the Chicago lakefront, which is near my office. A couple of weeks later, he passed away, having been able to maintain physical strength and a positive attitude right up until the end of his life. Stories like this should remind us that we can strive to live fully, optimistically, and expressively now, regardless of what health challenges we are currently facing or may face in the future.

Keep in mind that your health story is always co-written with Source: you can't control every aspect of it. You might develop a disease or condition that reduces your quality and length of life, yet you might find you can manage its symptoms better than you might expect and live considerably longer than the prognosis you were given. At some point, you might decide to revise the story of your health to acknowledge any changes that have occurred. A more realistic story for you might make it easier for you to feel comfortable with the balance between what you can change and what you have to accept.

Aging, Health Stories, and Themes

It bears repeating that only a quarter of people over age 65 experience memory loss. Only 14 percent can no longer drive safely. And people over 75 tend to report feeling younger than they did at 65. These statistics, reported in the *Wall Street Journal,*[4] contradict many of the negative stories we hear about aging and health. Discouraging stories about aging are embedded in movies and news reports, and they are reinforced by attitudes we encounter when talking with other people who have internalized these narratives. Similarly, the stories we hear about cancer, diabetes, multiple sclerosis, and other serious diseases often are negative, focused on loss and suffering rather than on living well despite these challenges.

Yet a story about living with cancer can be a story about discovering one's true calling, overcoming past trauma, building community, and developing a sense of purpose and meaning. A story about living with the aches and pains of aging can be a story about overcoming a tendency toward pessimism and becoming more optimistic in later life. If your health story had a chapter on aging, what would its themes be? Acceptance, resistance, or denial? Pride, embarrassment, or adventurousness?

What words summarize your beliefs about aging?

I dread being seen as over the hill, irrelevant, and past my prime.
I'm afraid of losing my looks and being seen as no longer attractive.
You can't teach an old dog new tricks.
I'm going to fight aging every way I can.
I won't grow old before my time!
I'm not getting older. I'm getting better.
As long as my doctor gives me a clean bill of health annually,
I don't want to think about getting older.

Health challenges commonly experienced during the process of aging—pain, weakness, breathing difficulties, loss of flexibility, and so on—do not have to be central to the health stories we write for ourselves. New themes such as perseverance, lightheartedness, and curiosity can take the place of themes like suffering, fear, and victimhood.

Sometimes, new health concerns arise and health conditions worsen. As you look back at your health story's themes about managing the symptoms of a condition, you may see similarities to the themes of aging. Are those themes working for you, or would you like to change them?

For example, would you like to dialogue with your resistance to aging to discover how it is affecting your health? "I'm not going to grow old before my time" may be a positive belief for you, but you may be unaware of some of the ways resistance to aging may be negatively affecting you.

Denying that you have experienced recent physical weaknesses or imbalances that could be symptoms of a developing condition is one example of how your resistance might be a problem for you. Checking out those possible symptoms might help you to arrest or even reverse a health problem while denial and resistance might result in further deterioration. Perhaps you need a different relationship with your resistance to aging, one that is more positive for you. Then, too, you might discover you need to work with a theme of acceptance or honesty.

Are you uncomfortable with your health story? Is your health story realistic for you, and if not, do you want to revise it? It can be very hard to retain habits you wanted to incorporate into your new story—and hard to get rid of old ones that do not work for you anymore.

You can research different approaches to addressing your health challenges and set new goals as part of a new health story. Even so, you will surely have days when it seems the new health story you wrote is not manifesting as expected. Accessing the insights and energies available to you in your unconscious may not be enough to restore your previous state of health or significantly slow degenerative processes in your body. Perhaps the health story you wrote for yourself is no longer realistic and you realize you would like to write a new one in which you accept your limitations. Perhaps you have underestimated how much better your health story could be, and you would like to improve it even more. If so, you might wish to do the following journaling exercise for revising your health story.

JOURNALING EXERCISE: REVISING YOUR HEALTH STORY

When you wrote your new health story earlier, I encouraged you to be ambitious and optimistic about what you might be able to experience. Reread what you wrote. Then, reflect on it by answering the following questions in your journal.

- If you have begun to bring to life your new health story, are any aspects of it not working for you? If so, what are they?
- Are you experiencing the changes you hoped to experience? If not, why do you think that is?

- What themes are evident in your health story right now? For example, are you experiencing resistance, impatience, or denial? Would you like to change the themes of your health story? If so, what themes might you prefer? What archetypal energies might help you to bring in these new themes?
- Are you struggling to change certain habits? What have you learned about those habits? Are you open to doing more work with your unconscious mind to address your failure to change certain habits?
- Are there habits you could change by substituting a better, healthier habit? For example, if you eat an unhealthy food before bed or after work in order to relax and reward yourself, is there something else you could do that would give you a sense of relaxation and reward?
- Is a shortage of quality sleep affecting your mood and energy? Do you need the new story of your health to incorporate more sleep, rest, and down time? What would it look like if you were to rest more and stop pushing yourself so much? Are you afraid that bringing to life a new story of your health will involve too much work and will wear you out?
- Looking back at the new health story you wrote for yourself, is it realistic for you? And does it have to be realistic? Are there benefits to having an "unrealistic" and ambitious new story of your health? If so, what are those benefits?
- Are there any expanded-awareness practices in this book you would now like to use to access the wisdom and energies in your unconscious? For example, would you like to encounter and work with your resistance, your denial, and habits you are having trouble breaking, and so on?

Let's say you were ambitious when writing your new health story and made a goal to lose 30 pounds and keep it off. You have improved your eating and exercise habits, you have lost five pounds and kept them off, but now are wondering if your goal was realistic. You might want to use techniques and strategies that help you remain mindful of your behavior so that you stick with the habits you have chosen for yourself, such as eating more vegetables at every meal, doing aerobic exercise almost every day, or building muscle mass to burn more calories. You might wish to make small improvements to help you lose more weight. Perhaps you will never reach your goal of losing 30 pounds and keeping it off, but maybe you can lose 10, or even more, if you alter your health story and bring it to life.

Your story about health might have a theme of impatience because it is taking a long time for you to recover from an injury or to lose unwanted weight. Setbacks may upset you greatly because you are impatient. You might need to confront your impatience and learn from it, perhaps by setting an intention to dialogue with it to learn more. You might also want to dialogue with your excess weight, your cancer or condition, or your inner healer. Let your intuition guide you in choosing which of these you most would like to ask questions of and listen to, and consider dialoguing with all of them to see if you get different insights.

If you discover you are struggling with whether or not to resist or accept your health condition, keep in mind that acceptance does not mean giving up entirely when it comes to sustaining or improving your current level of health. Impatience can keep you mindful of what your current health story is and whether it needs to be changed. If you are dissatisfied with your health story, you can always revise it. However, it may be that what you need is not to change your health story but your relationship with patience. It may have much to teach you.

When changing your health story, you might want to consider the theme of immunity. Are you doing what is necessary to maintain not just a strong immune system in your body but a strong psychological immune system that allows you to handle mental and emotional stressors? Then, too, spiritual challenges, such as feeling a lack of purpose or a sense of meaning, are more tolerable if you have a strong spiritual immune system, that is, you regularly feel a connection to Source and your own spirituality. When your spiritual immune system is strong, you recognize your energetic nature, respect it, and make choices that promote immunity within your energy field.

One way to have greater immunity within your energy field is through cleansing your energy body. As I said, I hope you will do this before using the expanded-awareness practices in this book that involve shifting your consciousness, but you might also consider doing it regularly. Any spiritual practice that helps you to get in touch with your personal energy field, clear it of blockages, and bring in replenishing light can contribute to spiritual and energetic immunity and may help you to avoid developing ailments in your physical body.

Earlier in the book, you learned about chakras, the energy vortexes that extend from the energy field that surrounds your physical body into your body at points that have been identified in ancient wisdom traditions. The following chakra-cleansing practice can help you to optimize the functioning of your chakras and improve your energetic immunity. It's possible that such an energetic tune-up could help you maintain physical immunity as well. I have used this practice often to improve my own health and well-being and to ensure that the health story I want to live according to is energized.

EXPANDED-AWARENESS PRACTICE: CLEANSING YOUR CHAKRAS

Lie down and draw your attention to your first or root chakra, located in your groin at the base of your spine. Begin cleansing the chakra, or energy vortex, by using your dominant hand.

Let your middle fingers hang a few inches above your groin, pointing down at your body, a few inches above it, and then use them to draw any heavy, disordered energy out of the middle of the spinning chakra.

Do this by moving your fingers in a circular motion, counterclockwise (as if there were a clock face there, facing the ceiling). Perform this cleansing action several times. Use your fingers to gather the energetic debris and flick it away from your energy field, imagining that it is being returned to the earth. Use your intuition to decide when the chakra is cleared of energetic debris. Then, reach up and bring in the pure white light of Source into your hand, and put it into that chakra. When you are finished, use your fingers to spin your first chakra clockwise, setting it back in motion clockwise—the direction it is meant to spin.

Continue working your way up through all seven chakras, cleansing and reinvigorating each one in this way, moving from the second chakra (located just below your navel) to your third or solar plexus chakra (just below your rib cage), to the fourth (at the center of your body, parallel to your heart), fifth (at your throat), sixth or third eye (at the middle of your forehead), and seventh (at the crown of your head).

After cleansing your chakras, you might journal about what you experienced. Did you feel any emotions while doing this exercise? Did you pick up on the energies of your chakras? Did you experience sensations, and if so, what do you make of them? Did you receive any messages about your energy field or your health? How did you feel when you finished compared with when you started?

Immunity protects you against external threats to your health and well-being that come into your body or, from a shamanic perspective, into your energy field. It is also important to be honest with yourself about the things you are doing that are not supporting your new health story.

Denial and Small Choices That Add Up

Making conscious choices to act differently is easier when you identify obstacles, small or large, that challenge you. Denial can get in the way of addressing health issues that may be easier to influence than you realize. If you notice the small choices you are making that are in conflict with the health story you wish to experience, and you acknowledge that they add up to obstacles you are creating, you will have a better chance of bringing your new health story to life.

Sometimes, denial happens simply because we are not paying attention to the contrast between what we say we want to do and what we actually do. When I've tried to make changes to my health story, I have been surprised to find many of my choices were automatic and mindless. In my office, we often have a bowl of candy or pretzels filled with peanut butter in the reception area, along with other snacks people have brought in to share with their coworkers.

I used to find it easy to avoid many of these snacks because I wasn't hungry, but those peanut-butter-filled pretzels seemed to call my name whenever I was walking by. It was hard to have just a few. Popping a few pretzels into my mouth does not immediately lead to poor health outcomes. However, small choices made again and again have a cumulative effect. I did not want my health story to include overeating, yet here I was, doing it a few fatty, sugary snacks at a time.

When I became aware of how often I was eating these snacks throughout the day, and over the course of a week, I made a conscious choice to avoid looking at the bowl where they tend to appear. I am able to rely on my willpower in those moments when I walk by them now. The point is not to berate yourself for bad choices; it's to recognize your patterns and shift them incrementally.

How often are you reaching into the pretzel bowl, skipping a daily walk, or otherwise violating your commitment to changing your health habits? Are you aware of the small choices you are making that add up? Establishing new habits sometimes can be as simple as recognizing a bad habit and substituting a better one. Stretching whenever you are about to pass through the reception area, and taking the time to smile and say hello to your coworker, might be a substitute for mindlessly fishing a snack out of a bowl.

As you work to change habits, you might find it helpful to pair the new habit you would like to develop with a pleasant activity or experience. Listening to enjoyable music or looking out the window at a beautiful scene while doing stretches might actually make you look forward to doing them.

Can you make it easier to engage in a new habit? What can you do to reduce any cues that tend to make you fall back into the old habit?

For example, if you typically collapse onto your couch after a long day at work, and remain there for an hour or so, can you make it harder to plop down and turn on the television? Could you cover your couch with items you would have to clear before sitting on it? What about keeping your remote inconveniently far away? Could you place a journal and pen on your couch before you leave home for the day, so that you return to a reminder that you want to get some exercise and journal before dinner?

Increasingly, people are using mobile devices and applications (apps) to remind them to engage in activities they would like to establish as habits. A friend of mine noticed her phone has an app that tells her how many steps she has walked during the day. While she had not intended to count her steps, she now regularly checks her phone to see how many steps she has walked; she feels motivated to increase her numbers when she sees the number is low compared with the day before. You might want to do something similar and even reward yourself in small ways for sticking to your goal when you haven't yet experienced long-term payoffs. Rewards might include treating yourself to a movie, concert, or a day off from work spent indulging in a hobby.

Some small changes will take more effort to bring about, and you might come to realize you are in denial of how often you say "no" to the new habit and "yes" to the old one. Denial about how much you are resisting changes will make it even harder to take control of your health story, rewrite it, and bring the new story to life. You might wish to regularly reflect on how you are meeting your health challenges, how you are feeling about them, and what your beliefs are. You can overcome denial by attending support group meetings, journaling, and using techniques for encountering insights and energies in transpersonal realms.

Are you aware of the limitations of your willpower? This source for establishing and maintaining new habits may not be enough when extra time, mental energy, and preparation are needed for new habits to stick. Let's say you realize you must attend to your health several times a day because you have developed a disease or condition requiring considerable attention. You might resent the amount of energy it takes to keep track of doctors' appointments and medications you need to take. You might feel tired of struggling to maintain your health. You might resist changes in your health story that you did not anticipate, and deny how serious your condition is and how much effort it takes for you to manage it. It can help to explore your emotional resistance to the fact that you have lost some control over your health story. Facing your resistance and better understanding it may lead you to feel more motivated and optimistic, and may even lead to a change in habits and a new health story.

If you find yourself repeatedly choosing to take actions that are not in synch with the new health story you wrote, perhaps you have a deep resistance to bringing that story to life. Maybe you are holding on to guilt or shame, which is preventing you from feeling entitled to experience better health. You might want to use some of the expanded-awareness practices to learn why you are continuing to feel that you do not deserve to experience wellness. You might dialogue with your shame or low self-esteem or your inner healer to learn more.

Expanded-awareness practices can make it easier to overcome denial by helping you work through any shame or resistance to the truth about what you are experiencing and your role in it. They can also serve as mindfulness practices. Each time you open and close sacred space, cleanse your energy field, and focus on your breathing, you slow down your mental chatter and reduce its intensity.

Eventually, you develop greater mindfulness and self-awareness, which in turn allows a space to open up between the old habit and the moment of choice. At these points, you automatically notice you are facing a decision. You are able to slow down your natural reaction and consciously consider what your decision will be. This offers you greater power to break old patterns and say "yes" to the new health story and new habits you want to instill. Combined with willpower, mindfulness practice can make a significant difference in your ability to bring to life a new health story that does not include the old habits.

In revising your health story, you can dialogue with your resistance to making the changes you wanted to make. You can also dialogue with your weariness, frustration, or denial. Ask your inner healer what you can do to change a habit. For example, you might ask it what you need to let go of, aside from the habit itself. You might be holding on to a habit out of a sense of shame or fear that if you do revise your health story, there will be negative consequences you are not prepared for. There can be payoffs to being unhealthy, as you contemplated when doing the journaling work to identify your current health story.

As you use the practices in this book and become more aware of the relationship between your body and your unconscious beliefs, feelings, and thoughts, you may find it easier to notice when your body is creating psychosomatic illness in order to experience benefits, such as increased attention from others or a break from your responsibilities. You will find it easier to dialogue with your hidden resistance and may feel that, for the first time, you have become empowered to reduce its influence on your health story.

When You Discover Your Ailment Is Psychosomatic

Psychosomatic ailments and illnesses are nothing to be ashamed of. Instead, they should be seen as opportunities for learning more about how to become empowered to tell a new story—of your health, and perhaps, of your life, too.

A woman named Sonya went to visit her elderly mother in a city far from her home. Her mother, Elizabeth, had just developed some serious health issues related to aging, and Sonya began to recognize for the first time just how difficult it would be for her mother to retain her independence, given her health condition. Sonya's brother spoke with her on the phone, and the two agreed that he would fly out and help her make arrangements for their mother to get a higher degree of care.

Sonya was sleeping in Elizabeth's living room when the doorbell rang, and she realized it was her brother, who had just come from the airport. Instantly, her back went into spasm. Elizabeth went to the door and let her son in while her daughter, Sonya, lay immobilized by the severe cramping of her back. Sonya recognized the psychosomatic muscle spasm was very real, in that she could not move without severe pain, yet it was also related to the fact that being unable to move made her brother instantly begin taking on the role of caretaker.

As she listened to and participated in the family conversation, Sonya realized she was going to be able to depend on her brother in the weeks and months ahead, and her back muscles relaxed. Her body seemed to realize that the burden of caretaking would not be entirely on her back, so it stopped resisting the fact that she would have to make changes in her life to be able to perform caretaking duties for her mother.

Afterward, Sonya reflected upon how much she had been in denial of the signs of deterioration her mother had been reporting over the phone for many months. The reality of the situation, which she could no longer deny when actually with Elizabeth, had triggered an intense unconscious resistance. Sonya realized she needed to begin dealing with her new story of being the daughter of a mother who was aging and who might need more of her daughter's attention, time, and support in the years to come.

In a situation such as this, I would encourage a client to dialogue with her fears about caretaking and her own health, especially given that caretakers often develop health concerns of their own as a result of focusing so much on another person and not processing their difficult emotions about the situation. As always, what you dialogue with is up to you, but every time you dialogue you can deepen your understanding of what you need to learn in order to optimize your health story.

Caretaking can be very challenging. Working as a therapist or physician and not being affected by patients' emotions can be difficult, too. You may not realize how much your connection with those who are suffering is affecting your own health story. Could you be in denial about aspects of your own health story, and how it has been, is, or will be affected by caretaking responsibilities? Are you neglecting your body as a result of caretaking?

Habits That Are Addictions

One reason we can overlook our role in our health problems, and the truth about any negative habits, is that we enjoy the short-term payoffs of pleasure and feeling good physically. We know we are neglecting our long-term health, but it is hard to stay focused on any distant negative consequences.

The following journaling exercise may be helpful for getting past denial and resistance to the idea that you have negative health habits you need to change, or that you have developed an addiction.

JOURNALING EXERCISE: IDENTIFYING HABITS AND ADDICTIONS

Answer the following questions in your journal.

- What habits, if any, are you having trouble breaking?
- How often could you say no to an old habit in a moment of choice and still feel you are enjoying life? Could you completely end the habit? Could you say no to the old habit more often so you gradually break it?
- Do you believe you have an addiction? How might you determine whether you have one? Would you be willing to take the next step in learning whether or not you have an addiction?
- Are you being too hard on yourself about your imperfections? If so, what do you need to do to let go of your perfectionistic tendencies?
- If you have an addiction, or fear that you will develop one, what do you need to do to break or prevent that addiction? What supports do you need for resisting the addictive substance, food, or behavior? What might you do to bring those supports into your story?
- What have you learned from journeying and dialoguing about your addiction or your resistance to change, or both? What journeys, dialogues, practices, and exercises do you want to use to learn more and change the archetypal energies affecting you?
- If you have sought short-term payoffs and ignored long-term consequences, what are some of the long-term positive payoffs to breaking your habits and overcoming your addictions? Can you write them out and remind yourself of them daily?

As you look at your health story again and begin to think about whether you want to revise it further, you may find yourself thinking about your future and how your health story might change in ways you can't control. What will happen if you make no more changes to your health story and habits and continue living as you are? You might not like the consequences of your choices. Working with your unconscious, you can get past your denial and start to deal with the future today, revising your health story according to what you learn about the road ahead.

I said earlier that shamans work with the future to do healing work in the present. The following expanded-awareness practice is derived from a practice used by healers among the Quechua, the indigenous people of Peru. Like the lower world journey, the upper world journey is believed to be an experience in a transpersonal realm. In this case, however, instead of getting to the origins of your challenges by looking at the past, as you did in the lower world journey, you will be looking to the future to learn what changes you need to make in your health story today so that your future health story will be better.

The upper world is associated with immortal beings, celestial spirit guides, and the future. It contains numerous possibilities for your path through this lifetime. Shamans might visit the upper world to connect with universal energies that have the power to help actualize a desired future.

Journeys to this realm, the world of your becoming, can give you symbols and insights to energize you to take actions in the present more in keeping with the best destiny you and Source can create together. The upper world journey also allows you to change the energies that are affecting your health story.

In the transpersonal realms, which is where you will go on this journey, the past, present, and future exist simultaneously. One reason to take the upper world journey is that energies that exist in the future may be drawing you forward on a trajectory that will take you to an undesired outcome. This journey lets you change that trajectory. In fact, you might think of the upper world journey as taking you through a process of diagnosis, prognosis, and treatment and then revealing to you what the outcome will be.

The diagnosis involves observing what is really happening in your health story versus what you wish were happening. You dissolve the obstacle of denial and become aware of what was hidden from your conscious mind. The prognosis involves seeing the trajectory of your health story if you make no changes. The treatment consists of discovering what you must do to change your trajectory and your prognosis and then applying those insights to your everyday life. The upper world journey can help you revise your health story rather than continue to pretend it is something different.

As this is a detailed journey, you might wish to record the instructions and play them back to guide you. If you do this, be sure to leave pauses in the recording to allow plenty of time for insights to appear after you take an action, such as entering a chamber or asking a question.

Prepare for this exercise by setting your intention to journey to the upper world to gain insights and energy for transforming your health story. Then, open sacred space, cleanse your energy field, and breathe mindfully.

EXPANDED-AWARENESS PRACTICE: JOURNEY TO THE UPPER WORLD

Imagine you see before you a mountain that you will ascend easily, winding your way up a trail clockwise toward its summit, which is drawing you to it energetically. Know that this mountain holds great wisdom for you at its peak, and feel yourself preparing to open to all it can offer you.

Here, you will discover insights that can be tremendously helpful in bringing to life a new health story, one that will help you to experience the best possible health you can as the future unfolds. The energies on this mountaintop can enter your energy body and alter it in positive ways.

Feel yourself traveling along the winding road toward the top of the mountain. Feel your courage as you open up to what you will discover.

Let your energy body slow its ascent and come to a stop before the first of four chambers or caves within the mountain (on your right). Just outside this first chamber, notice a guardian, your inner healer, and how it appears to you.

Ask it, "Is now a good time for me to make this journey to the upper world?" If the answer is no, ask, "What do I need to do before being able to continue this journey?" Wait for the answer. You can do what your inner healer asks, or negotiate with it, or decide to come back another day, knowing your inner healer is an aspect of yourself that wants to protect you from undue emotional and psychological stress.

If you decide to end the journey for today, return down the winding road to the base of the mountain and thank your inner healer before returning to ordinary reality. If you are continuing the journey, turn your attention to the first chamber.

Standing before this first chamber, pose the question, "What will my health be in the future if I make no changes now?" (If you like, you can pick a specific time in the future, such as 5 years from now, or 10.)

Pause and wait for the moment in which you know you are to enter this chamber along with your inner healer, who will guide you on this journey and be an ally supporting you. You might see the door open, or you might open it yourself.

Alternatively, you might see a light beckoning to you to come forth and step into the presence of the wisdom and energies you seek. Regardless of how you are beckoned, step forward when you recognize it is time to do so. Observe what you are experiencing and what insights arise in your awareness.

Then, turn to your inner healer and ask, "Is there anything else I should see here before I depart?" Follow its guidance. It may point out to you something you missed here in the chamber. When you are ready, depart from the chamber.

Continue your ascent along the winding mountain trail with your guardian still accompanying you, toward the second chamber. When you are in front of it, ask, "What do I need to let go of to improve my health so I will not experience what I just saw?"

When you are ready, enter with your inner healer and receive the answer. Turn again to your inner healer, and ask if there is anything else you need to see in this chamber.

Then leave the chamber with your guardian, and wind your way up the trail to the third chamber. Before entering, ask, "What do I need to gain to improve my health in the future so that the picture I just saw in the first chamber will not be what I experience?"

Go into the chamber and wait to receive the answer. Then ask your inner healer if there is anything else you should see before you move on. Follow its guidance. Depart the chamber, or remain there and explore it further, until you become aware that it is time to continue on to the fourth and final chamber.

Ascend the road to the fourth chamber and, when you are ready, ask, "If I make the changes I just learned about, what will my health look like in the future?"

Enter the chamber with your inner healer, and wait for an answer. Follow its guidance. Depart from the chamber, or remain there and explore it further, until you sense it is time to leave.

Exit the chamber and descend the mountain trail. Pause, feeling the changes you experienced, accepting the wisdom you have taken in.

Then thank the energies of the four chambers for helping you, and your inner healer for being your ally.

Close sacred space. Journal about your experience and apply the lessons to your everyday life so that you can alter your health story.

A man named Jon used the upper world journey to discover where he would be in 10 years if he made no health changes. He reported that in the first chamber, he saw himself as an old, decrepit man. It was an upsetting image, but he continued the journey anyway. In the second chamber, he learned that he needed to let go of his ideas about the inevitability of bad aging if he was going to change the trajectory he was on.

In the third chamber, he learned that he needed to gain a positive attitude to change his future health story. In the fourth chamber, he saw himself as an older man, but this time, the future self he observed seemed to have a greater sense of well-being, a better attitude, and a more youthful energy. He brought from that future self the energy of well-being and vitality, so that he could experience them in the present.

Although Jon knew intellectually that there were benefits to adopting and maintaining a positive attitude about growing older, his knowledge had not led him to change his fears or resistance to growing older. His negative beliefs and feelings about aging had been deep-rooted. Recognizing how powerful his hidden beliefs were, and how they were leading him down a road he did not wish to travel, he became more committed to doing the work of changing his health story and his beliefs about how he would experience aging. His journey to the upper world helped him to start changing.

Jeff, another man who took the upper world journey, reported that in the first chamber, he saw himself in a wheelchair, his legs having been amputated due to diabetes, and he recognized that his future self was on kidney dialysis. In the second chamber, he discovered he needed to let go of his habit of bargaining. He often told himself he should go ahead and enjoy eating sweets or skip testing his blood sugar, reasoning that he would do it "next time," but he would respond to the temptation in the same way just about every time. He wasn't living up to the bargains he was making because he was saying yes to sweets far more often than he was saying no, and skipping the important task of frequently testing his blood sugar. The result was uneven blood sugar levels that he knew were causing invisible damage to his body at a cellular level.

It might seem contradictory that he had to let go of a bad habit (bargaining) *and* accept himself; however, accepting oneself can mean being honest about one's failings and weaknesses. When shame prevents self-reflection and self-honesty, changing bad habits can be very difficult.

In the third chamber, Jeff learned that he needed to develop the discipline to stick to his plan to change his health habits. While he knew this intellectually, experiencing the message within the third chamber touched him powerfully. In the fourth chamber, he saw he would be more accepting of his diabetes and manage it better in the future. He was not in a wheelchair, was not having his legs amputated, and was not receiving kidney dialysis. After this experience, Jeff might have continued his work on writing and bringing to life a new health story by dialoguing with his shame or his chronic condition, or he might have chosen to work with the archetypal energy of endings.

The Archetypal Energy of Endings
(The Death Principle)

In revising your health story, and reckoning with such archetypal energies as resistance and acceptance, it can be helpful to use an expanded-awareness practice that will allow you to energetically release something that is no longer working for you. You might release a negative attitude, a fear, or a habit. One way to do this is by working with the archetypal energy of endings, sometimes known as the death principle. If you engage this archetypal energy, learn from it, and let it assist you energetically, you may find the courage to break away from old habits of mind, heart, and body. You may even feel born into a new sense of possibility as a result. You might need to work with the energy of endings several times before you feel you have truly rid yourself of something you wanted to release.

Start this journey with an intention to encounter and receive assistance from the energy of endings. Prepare by opening sacred space, cleansing your energy field, and doing mindful breathing.

EXPANDED-AWARENESS PRACTICE: JOURNEY TO ENCOUN-TER THE ENERGY OF ENDINGS

Envision a long corridor before you that has a doorway at the end, with a door that opens to a room where the energy of endings resides. Begin to walk down the corridor. Notice how you feel and any images or sensations coming up for you. If you feel resistance, tell yourself, "I am only going to end what I choose to end."

You retain the power to choose to let something in your life die. The energy of endings is simply your ally.

Continue down the corridor until you reach the door. Open it, and step inside a chamber where you meet the energy of endings. Greet this energy, and notice how it greets you. Observe the form that the energy of endings takes.

Ask, "What do I need to know in order to revise my health story to be more satisfactory to me?" Let the dialogue continue.

At some point, ask, "What do I need to release or let die?" As you dialogue with the energy of endings, remember to ask it, too, what it can give you to bring back into your life so you can live according to a better health story. Dialogue as long as you are receiving helpful messages.

When the dialogue is complete, thank the energy of endings for its assistance. Leave the room, and close the door. Then, return down the long hallway to where you began.

Close sacred space. Write in your journal about your experiences, and apply to your life whatever wisdom you have gained.

When encountering the energy of endings, it is common to learn that you need to let go of a habit, an emotion, or even a relationship with something or someone. You might need to end your relationship with sugary treats, or with the habit of making excuses for eating sugary foods.

You could meet with the energy of endings again and have another dialogue to get more information and to see if you come back from the encounter feeling it is easier to avoid sugar. Checking in with yourself after using a practice is always a good idea because you may wish to use a different practice to see if you achieve better results.

Also, you can use the following cord-cutting practice to help you energetically release what is not serving you, whether it is a relationship to a person or to a habit, experience, or substance. Before you begin, set your intention to energetically release something that is no longer serving you. If you like, open sacred space, cleanse your energy field, and do mindful breathing to prepare for the practice.

EXPANDED-AWARENESS PRACTICE: CORD CUTTING

Imagine there is a cord extending from your physical body, right though your energy body, out to whatever it is you no longer want to be connected to. Notice the cord pulsing as energy is exchanged between you and this thing. Now, imagine the cord is being cut.

The energy stops flowing from your end of the cord, and the energy coming to you from what was connected to you stops flowing. Then, as you inhale, the cord that extends from you gently recoils back into you.

As this happens, feel the energy that was in the cord—and flowing out of you—being reabsorbed into your body. As you exhale, the energy that was flowing into you is expelled and starts to be reabsorbed by whatever is its source.

When you are ready, come back into ordinary consciousness.

After you have done the cord-cutting exercise, close sacred space if you opened it. Later, journal about your experience. Notice whether your new health story is becoming easier to maintain and what effect, if any, the exercise might have had. You might wish to use this practice several times and see if it makes a difference in your sense of having released something. What will come in to replace what you released? You may not yet know what it is, but by using other expanded-awareness practices in this book, you can discover the answer.

Challenges to Your New Health Story

Earlier, you did an exercise in which you examined your habits and considered whether you have an addiction. It is possible to replace an unhealthy habit or addiction with a healthy habit, only to have that new healthy habit turn into an obsession. In a case such as this, inflexibility and fear of slipping back into the old ways can cause stress for you and for your friends and family.

You might want to dialogue with your inflexibility, or you could dialogue with your inner healer to learn more about how to maintain your new habits, even when you are being triggered to slip back into the old ways. Working with the energy of endings, perhaps doing the journey described earlier and then using a cord-cutting exercise a few times, might help you feel more confident that you have put the old habits behind you. Even so, you know what your limitations are. You might not be able to handle family gatherings where people are drinking. You might have to take yourself away from the holiday table full of food when the meal is over. Know what works for you, and be conscious of your triggers and your fears of returning to your old habits, and your obsessions and inflexibility may be much reduced.

Emotional stressors, self-defeating thoughts, and physical stressors such as not getting enough rest can be triggers for old habits that once gave you comfort. Consider how you might be able to address these challenges, and have some plans in place for especially challenging situations.

You might come up with some new ways to get movement and exercise that alleviate stress, or you might find new means for relaxation or for changing your self-talk. Simple interventions for stress, such as putting on some music and dancing, lifting free weights or doing stretches a few times a day, or performing some yoga poses while looking out a window at your backyard, could make a difference in your ability to manage stress that triggers old habits. You might take a walk and think about your self-talk that is supporting stress rather than well-being, and why you ruminate. You might journal about that, too, and have a dialogue with your inner healer to learn more.

Health by the Numbers

One simple way to manage your obsessions about health and be more flexible is to track your health numbers. When you come to see that you are keeping within a range of healthy numbers for weight, BMI, steps walked, blood pressure, and so on, you may find it easier to let go of obsessing over your health and any fear of slipping back into the old ways.

How do your health numbers look? When a nurse tells you what your blood pressure is, or when you step on a scale, does the number affect your outlook for the day? Health apps and activity trackers have become popular lately, in part because we tend to look to numbers to tell us how to feel about our health. Naturally, we want to see whether we are doing well at maintaining our health or even improving it. A weight gain of a pound or two or "bad" numbers on a medical test can wake us up to the need to change our health habits, which is good. But it is possible to give too much emphasis to numbers and end up feeling demoralized by them instead of inspired to change. Then we may simply start to avoid looking at our numbers—or obsess about them but not put energy into figuring out what to do differently and how to get it done. Looking at the numbers on your scale but not making changes to your eating and exercise habits is a waste of time.

Big changes can be very difficult, but you can set small goals and establish new habits so as to experience less stress and better health and wellness. Small successes can then inspire larger goals. You could eliminate a second glass of wine with dinner, and skip wine altogether a few nights a week, and watch your numbers on the scale change. When you get into your car to drive to or from work, you could consciously choose to meditate for several minutes before starting your engine and, over time through meditation, retrain your brain and even reshape it to be less emotionally reactive to potentially stressful situations. You could walk outdoors in nature for a few minutes a day, thereby lowering your levels of the stress hormone cortisol and boosting your immunity, even as your mood lifts from being outdoors. You could set a goal to walk 10,000 steps at least once a week, or 8,500 steps three times a week, and when that goal has been met, increase it slightly.

One way to make numbers work in your favor is to record them whenever you look at lab tests results or your activity tracker's or scale's display. Notice what is your most common range of numbers. Maybe, instead of becoming upset that you gained two pounds, you will see that your weight fluctuates and, due to changes you have made in your daily habits, your range of weight is two pounds less than it was before, and you never hit that top number. Maybe, you can track how many days you met your goal of sticking to your new healthy habit, instead of worrying about not having reached the number you are seeking.

If when tracking the numbers you become frustrated by your slow progress, you might track different measures, such as how many days a month you met your goal. This week, you might do better than last week.

You might also pay closer attention to how it feels when you meet your goal. Small victories can inspire bigger ones. Minor setbacks can simply awaken you to the need to figure out how you got off track, and your insights can help you get back on track and stay there. If your downfall is longing for a reward for a hard day, maybe you can find a better reward than a glass of wine before dinner or a bowl of ice cream before bed.

If you have become obsessed with numbers, keep in mind that the numbers are just representations of health. They are not you. Do not overidentify with them and write a story for your health called, "I'm a failure because I can't get those numbers to budge." Do something differently. When you find your moods are affected by your numbers being "good" or "bad," you might be giving them too much influence over you. Do your numbers matter, or do you simply need to go about the business of living healthfully and improving your habits? Do you need to dialogue with acceptance, and write a new health story in which you are the weight you are? Do you need to research what you can do to make your health numbers change?

How can you move from obsession with the numbers to focusing on other issues regarding your health and feel more relaxed as you go about your activities of living, including the actions you take to change your health habits? You might start by writing a new story for yourself that goes beyond achieving certain numbers. Your new health story could be:

I am strong in my body, and it supports me in all I choose to do.
Sometimes I do not reach my exercise goals, but I choose not to worry and, instead, simply try again tomorrow.
I have noticed I have habits that don't serve my health, and I am changing them. I am optimistic about my potential for significant changes for the better.

How would it feel to free yourself from the tyranny of health indicator numbers and to create a new relationship with them? What would it be like if you were to say, "I'm just not going to pay attention to the numbers for a while"?

If this prospect scares you or makes you feel at loose ends, you are not alone. You may need to work on trusting yourself more, and you may need to explore why you struggle with changing habits or perfectionism. Try liberating yourself from checking your numbers for a while, if it will not pose an immediate threat to your health. Journal about how you feel during this experiment. Pay attention to how your body feels. You might find your body is giving you the message, "Don't worry so much! Stop obsessing and lighten up!" If so, think about how you might monitor your numbers without creating stress while doing it.

Health is more than numbers, which are simply a means to help you decide what you want to change about your health habits and what you want to keep doing. Remember, you are the storyteller. Change the story of your health any time you wish.

CHAPTER NINE

Healing Partnerships and Communities

What role do others play in your healing and your health story? Can they partner with you or support you? Is being a healer to others part of your health story? Can your helping people actually lead *you* to greater well-being, better lifestyle habits, and improved health?

There are health benefits to being in relationships with kind and loving people who support your mental and emotional wellness, rather than in relationships with people whose behavior and treatment of you causes you stress—and even leads you to be so anxious, upset, or depressed that you set aside the habits that promote good health.

What if the story of your health included experiences such as working with healers who are attentive to you and your health—and having friends who help you stay motivated to get regular exercise and family members who support you in eating more healthfully?

The story of your health might include statements such as "I'm enjoying very good health, and I have many professional healers I can count on, and friends and family who support me, in my process of healthy aging." It might be "I'm the comeback kid, and whenever I fear that the cancer will return, I know that my new, healthy habits, my doctors, and my supportive community will help me to minimize the chances of that happening. I feel confident and happy about my health and my ability to stay healthy."

Whether you are solely interested in self-healing, or a healer who works with others as well as yourself, you now have many techniques you can use to gain energies for healing and insights that might be invisible to your conscious mind. You might answer some of the following questions in your journal, as you consider the role of others in your health story:

- What professionals have you partnered with to improve your health story? How have those partnerships worked out for you?
- Would you like to change the way you relate to the professionals you have worked with or are working with and, if so, what changes would you like? Do you want to dialogue with your inner healer, your difficulty talking honestly with your primary care doctor, or something else to learn more?
- When it comes to your relationships with other people, are you getting enough support for your new health story? What would you like to change about your relationships so that you feel you have more support? Would you like to meet and bring into your life new people who can support you in living according to a new health story? If so, where might you find those people?
- Would you like to become more involved with, or begin, a healing community? What might that look like? Can you identify anyone who might help you to develop this community?

Also, consider writing a story about the people who are a part of your new health story, and how they fit in. Again, you might want to simply use first-person, "I" language and the present tense, and write a few paragraphs affirming that "I am working with a nutritionist, along with my doctors, to ensure that my team of healers is monitoring the way food and nutrients are affecting my condition," "I am attending support group meetings of others who have my condition," and so on.

Expanded-awareness practices can be used in a group, and later, participants can share with everyone what they experienced. As always, do not be too quick to analyze experiences. Share your thoughts with each other, but know that later, after you have done a shamanic journey or fire ritual together (for example), new insights might come to you. These might build upon, clarify, or contradict the first thoughts you had about what you experienced.

If you are a healer, you can learn to journey on behalf of others. However, it is a great responsibility, and I encourage you to take it seriously enough to get well trained to do this sort of work. You can help others simply by guiding them to do this work on their own and report to you their insights and experiences, so that you can come to understand their health stories and health challenges and better help your clients.

Once, I was working with my wife, Pat, who was recovering from breast cancer and the effects of surgery, chemotherapy, and radiation treatments. She had an infection in a lumpectomy incision that was oozing. We worked together for healing, and I had the spontaneous image of me sitting under a tree, with a crystal in my hand, and a woman in a pool under a waterfall, who was also holding a crystal. I could see our two crystals were connected energetically, infusing each other with energy. I recognized that both crystals were exchanging energy with a crystal I was holding.

At the same time, following my suggestion, Pat was visualizing that her inner healer was mobilizing her immune system to attack the infection. Within less than an hour, Pat's wound stopped oozing—very soon after, it closed up.

A few months later, a pathologist checked Pat's breast again and detected more cancer. Pat and I did more healing work, where once again I spontaneously had the image of me under the tree and the woman in the pool that I'd had before. Pat was visualizing energies inside her destroying the cancer and then being expelled out of her body through her belly. Then she visualized healing blue-green light entering the places from which she had taken the cancer. She and I did this work together several times over the course of a few weeks.

Pat had been scheduled for a mastectomy because, according to the tests, chemotherapy and radiation and the lumpectomy had not removed all the cancer. As the date neared, she asked the surgeon to stop and do frozen C-sections (biopsies that show any cancerous growths) before removing her breast to be sure the cancer was, in fact, still present. While she was under anesthesia for the mastectomy, her surgeon ordered a number of frozen C-sections, and each time came out to show me that there was no trace of cancer. When Pat woke up from anesthesia, she realized she still had her breast. The surgeon explained that, indeed, the biopsies had shown she no longer had the cancer and did not need a mastectomy after all.

How much our energy work, separately and together, affected the outcome, I don't know. But the two of us felt that working together had been more effective than either of us working alone to help heal the wound and the cancer.

Dialoguing When a Healing Partnership Has Problems

As I said, the expanded-awareness practice of dialoguing should not be used with a figure that was or is a real person. If you are encountering problems in working with a healer who is helping you, or you are a healer and are having problems working with a client, you should have an actual dialogue with the person to sort out any issues. However, you might wish to dialogue with any of the following feelings you may have so you can gain more insights into the conflict between you and this other person:

- Your resentment of the person
- Your distrust of the person
- Your need to feel a sense of control
- Your resistance to authority and desire to rebel against it

The dialoguing technique will help you to learn more about what is hidden in your own unconscious that is interfering with the relationship. It could be that you need to let go of something or bring in something. It could be that you are in denial of your need to be more flexible, listen better, or take more responsibility for your choices. You might realize that while this person may be able to partner effectively with someone else, he or she is not a good partner for you at this time. Perhaps you will learn more about your healing practice and the types of clients you would like to attract to experience a greater sense of satisfaction. Or, you might come to realize what it is you need from a physician, alternative health healer, or psychologist to feel that your work with them is effective in helping you to heal. Be open to finding new partners in your health story.

A Healing Community

Your health story is connected to the health stories of others. As you change your health story and people see you as having more energy, looking better, and being less sick, they are likely to wonder what you are doing differently and what they can do to gain similar health results. You might feel drawn to share your story and even, perhaps, to study to become a healer yourself. If you are already a healer, you might decide to learn more about shamanism and Jungianism as modalities for healing that you could incorporate into your own work.

If you do not wish to formally study to become a healer or expand upon an existing healing practice, but wish to positively influence the health of others, there are other ways to do so. You might join or create a group devoted to healing through the use of expanded-awareness practices and journaling. Nature painting, in particular, can be a good way to get participants to go outdoors and do the work of releasing, replenishing, healing, and balancing.

The fire ceremony ritual can be used around a fire, with individuals taking turns placing sticks in the fire or doing it simultaneously. It can be interesting to see how the ceremony works and what happens spontaneously as participants use their intuition and tune in to each other as they choose when to step forward, speak, and add a stick to the fire. Afterward, you might wish to take turns spontaneously speaking a wish or prayer for the future.

These could be personal, universal, general, or specific. One person might say, "May all cancer patients receive the best possible medical treatment and support from their community"; another might say, "May I find ways to bring healthy foods onto my plate daily and develop the skill of vegetable gardening"; while another might say, "May my patients inspire me each day as I work at the healing center."

You can also join or start a group that meditates together or performs rituals, hosts workshops on healing, and so on, perhaps through your church, synagogue, or community center. You might want to attend health expos, lectures, and retreats.

If you are a medical professional and looking to learn more about how nutrition can enhance health, you could read research studies and attend workshops and conferences such as the annual Nutrition and Health Conference founded by Andrew Weil, MD.

You could also support your patients in using alternative and complementary treatments that could be of benefit to them. You could become an educator or trainer, bringing healing practices into schools and community centers, working with children and adults and teaching them tools for supporting a new health story. For example, you might volunteer to teach healthy cooking classes, yoga, or meditation.

You will always be in community with the earth and her creatures. How might you be sure that you are contributing? I believe the most important contribution is to consciously choose to tread lightly on the earth. If you think of the earth as a living being like yourself, you can imagine how billions of people straining her resources, adding toxins to her system, and not replenishing her or giving her time to heal could be very damaging.

When a human has an autoimmune disorder, that person's immune system doesn't recognize the body's own cells and attacks them as if they were dangerous intruders. Could the earth start to respond to us similarly? What new diseases might develop, and what natural disasters might occur, if we do not repair our relationship with the earth?

How might you live more gently on the earth? You could join a conservation group that removes invasive species plants from natural areas and carefully disposes of them. You could begin cultivating bees and butterflies in your yard or work at a nature center or school to do the same. In some communities, people plant vegetable gardens at apartment complexes, schools, or even on medians and traffic circles, and share their bounty with others. Some reclaim empty lots, replenishing the area with healthy soils so that the vegetables grown are of good quality.

In everyday life, be mindful of how your habits affect the earth. Small changes in your relationship with the earth matter. Tread softly, using eco-friendly transportation and practices. In this way, the earth will have a better health story, which in turn will contribute to a better health story for you—and your community.

Support for Health Challenges

Increasingly, hospitals and health care providers are coming to realize the power of community support for health challenges. If you are in need of such support and are unable to find it, start a group yourself simply by reaching out to one person you feel may be open to the idea.

Commonly, people join support groups when they are facing health challenges and, later, when they have written and brought to life a new health story, they continue on with the group. There is no reason to feel you must continue month after month, or year after year, however. If you sense it is time for you to become a part of a new healing community, use an expanded-awareness practice to learn more about transitioning from one to another.

For example, you may no longer want to be a part of a group of cancer survivors that mentor others undergoing cancer treatment, but you may find that you want to join or create a wellness community to help others live more healthful lives.

Community connections build immunity and seem to contribute to longer, healthier lives, so I encourage you to find ways to partner with others in co-writing new health stories. I also hope you will partner with healers who are not just skilled but attentive.

As I've been in more frequent contact with my doctors in order to address my health issues, I realize how valuable it is as a patient to have a doctor who takes extra time to answer questions, doesn't seem to be rushed, and doesn't treat you like another number that they need to hurriedly check off. On the other hand, I'm also struck by the fact that doctors are extremely busy people. They often work many hours and of course they, too, have lives, families, and obligations to themselves and others. Sometimes they have schedules that they can't control and they have to do more in a day than they counted on, which can create stress for them.

Physicians need to balance their medical pursuits with their need to get home and tend to other aspects of their lives that are important to them. Whenever I am unhappy with how a doctor treats me, I don't take the behavior personally. I figure that's just the way it is, given the pace and requirements of medical practices today.

Often doctors have not undergone some of the tests they administer and may not realize how painful or uncomfortable they can be. If they were to take on emotions their patients experience, they might become distracted or overwhelmed, so I try to keep that in mind. When they have experienced the conditions their patients have, or the treatments for those conditions, they respond with the same concerns, fears, denials, and defenses as the rest of us. Having seen this through my work with physicians who have developed cancer or other diseases, I am reminded that we're all in this together. We're all human, doing the best we can. Healers may themselves need healing so that they can better balance their desire to help others yet nourish themselves.

As I finish this book, I'm in a state of unknowing about some aspects of my health story. All I can do is work with the practices that I've suggested in this book and remember that my health story is part of the bigger story of my life, which is finite. I'm also reminded of the group stories I tell at the conclusion of each of my workshops. I start the story by saying, "Once upon a time, a group of people gathered to explore the stories of their health ..." I then look to the person on my left to continue the story, and they in turn hand it off to the next person, until the story comes back to me. Then I say, "And then suddenly ..."

The "suddenlys" in our lives come unexpectedly and can turn our lives upside down. But such is life. My hope is that by learning to relate to the transpersonal realms and your inner life, you can more artfully write the new story of your health in the midst of the "suddenlys." Now, you have the tools of expanded-awareness practices and journaling that can help you identify what you want to experience in your health story. Now, it will be easier to notice when you are tempted to fall back into old habits, and you may feel less drawn to engage in them. The exchanges of energy and information that are core to shamanic and Jungian techniques, and the framework of working with a story, are experiences I hope you have found helpful in your efforts to change the story of your health.

Going forward, I hope you will continue to use this book's techniques, not just for yourself but with others to help them in their quest for greater wellness. Many people need healing, and working with others can help them, and you, to feel a sense of community support as you step into a new way of relating to your health—through the power of story and the power of claiming your role as the storyteller.

Afterword

Evidence for the Effectiveness
and Promise of Energy Medicine

The mechanisms by which the mind affects the body are becoming more clear to us, as researchers look at the body's processes and make new discoveries about health and aging. The mind-body connection may turn out to be the key to our writing new health stories in the future. Expanded-awareness practices and energy medicine seem to hold great promise for healing.

Many physicians and medical experts in the West point to science and research to back their treatments. Yet there are limits to what research can tell us and its value in the world of clinical practice, much less the world of self-treatment. A cardiologist I heard speak said that less than half of what he does is based on evidence-based medicine—in other words, treatment based on what medical and scientific research shows to be the most effective interventions at the present moment in the understanding of a particular illness. Physicians who practice integrative and functional medicine are more likely to incorporate into their treatment a variety of modalities, or to refer you to healers who use non-Western methods of treatment.

Fortunately, many in the medical community are starting to reflect upon any biases they may have that conflict with the latest research. In an op-ed piece in the *New York Times*, regular columnist Aaron E. Carroll, MD, a professor of pediatrics at Indiana University School of Medicine, noted, "Too often, when confronted with evidence that advanced technology might not be providing benefits, the medical community refuses to change its behavior." As examples, he noted the overuse of mammography screening, advanced life support, and surgical procedures like arthroscopic surgery. At the same time, he pointed out that a meta-analysis of research on acupuncture found that placebo, or "sham," acupuncture (not actually using needles to treat the patient) shows it is *not* as effective as actual acupuncture, contradicting an argument that many have heard recently.[1]

Some who resist or dismiss energy medicine believe it only works due to the placebo effect and so-called "magical thinking." If any healers working with you feel this way, you might draw their attention to what Lissa Rankin, MD, author of *Mind Over Medicine: Scientific Proof That You Can Heal Yourself,* wrote in her blog:

> I question whether there's anything wrong with promoting "magical thinking."... I'm finding that promoting magical thinking is sometimes just what the doctor ordered. I'm NOT talking about misleading the patient or withholding necessary information. But I am talking about instilling in the patient the positive belief in the possibility of radical healing, even when the odds may go against a positive outcome.
>
> As I describe in *Mind Over Medicine,* in many ways, it was "magical thinking" (aka "hope") that helped me cut back from 7 medications to less than one...[2]

Increasingly, we are recognizing the power and complexity of the mind-body connection. We are exploring how we might use the mind to enhance treatment and management of disease and illness. We are even able to measure some of the effects of our mental/emotional activities on the body, such as measuring levels of the stress hormone cortisol. Over time, excess cortisol can lead to chronic inflammation, which plays a pivotal role in the development of diseases such as diabetes and Alzheimer's.

We know the placebo effect—the mind's ability to positively influence physical health through optimistic thoughts as well as emotions such as joy and gratitude—is strong. So, too, is the nocebo effect—the mind's ability to negatively influence physical health through fear and pessimism. These phenomena might hold promise for better, more effective treatments for health conditions. The field of epigenetics, or gene expression, holds promise for understanding how our experiences that are seemingly confined to the mental and emotional realm affect gene expression. Perhaps information and energies that affect us at a cellular level come not just from medications or obvious energetic influences (such as ultraviolet light or radiation), or from the mind and the power of its thoughts, but also from working with symbols that have energy. In her book *The Psyche of the Body*, Denise Gimenez Ramos notes that cancer cells have "impoverished information" that cause them to reproduce in an unhealthy way. She suggests that new information from medication and the placebo effect, and from work with symbols, might all be helpful for changing the cancer cells' behavior.[3]

We know that stress management techniques can reduce cortisol and adrenaline and boost immunity because the sympathetic nervous system is less often activated when stress management techniques are used regularly—and when it is activated, it is quickly counteracted by the parasympathetic nervous system. What if Jungian and shamanic techniques, and perhaps expanded-awareness practices such as chakra cleansing or working with nature to balance your energies, could turn on the parasympathetic nervous system and help your body recover from stress more quickly and effectively?

We do know that when our minds shift into a trancelike state, however we make that happen, the sympathetic nervous system stops being quite so active and allows the parasympathetic nervous system to come online.

The sympathetic nervous system within the human body responds to stress with what is meant to be a short-term alteration in breathing patterns, heart rate, and cortisol levels to enable us to escape danger. When it is chronically overactive, it lowers our immunity and increases cellular damage.

When the parasympathetic nervous system becomes activated, our heart rate slows, our breathing deepens, and our cortisol washes through our system—all of which contribute to greater immunity and to cellular repair. Different neurotransmitters (acetylcholine and serotonin), which are chemical messengers that help the brain do its job, are stimulated at this point. We experience improved mood, a sense of relaxation and happiness, and the perception of interconnectedness, along with improved immunity. When you are feeling emotionally stressed, run down, or sick, it makes sense to use expanded-awareness practices, whether they are the ones in this book or something else—for example, meditation or qigong.

Also, being in a trancelike state involves what Michael Winkelman, author of *Shamanism: A Biopsychosocial Paradigm*, calls "integrated brain processing." In integrated brain processing, the limbic system, a more primitive part of the brain associated with emotions, originates slow brain wave patterns that interact with the frontal cortex, the part of the brain where we form thoughts, plan actions, and analyze information. In other words, different areas of the brain have more communication with each other, creating coherent vibrations that harmonize with each other.[4]

Because brain waves are constantly being transmitted along the sheaths surrounding the nerve fibers that extend throughout the body, the coherent vibrations from the brain in this integrated processing state get transmitted to organs and cells. That, in turn, may facilitate healing of those structures in the body.

In addition, a brain in an integrated processing state may cause the body to release biochemicals called opioids, which reduce physical pain, and endorphins, which promote euphoria and better health in the short term and the long term. The physical and emotional relaxation that occurs enhances the body's ability to heal itself.

Some simple practices known to be emotionally relaxing can actually have significant effects on our body's health, cumulatively as well as immediately. In the short run, just 20 minutes of watching humorous videos has been shown to reduce cortisol levels (and sharpen memory).[5] Laughter stimulates circulation and increases how deeply you breathe, giving your system more oxygen. In the long term, it is known to reduce pain and boost immunity.[6] Even just anticipating that you will be amused releases endorphins.[7]

Cultivating a sense of playfulness and laughing more often may contribute to improved health and longevity. In fact, in a famous case of mind-body connection from years ago, writer Norman Cousins watched humorous movies, such as films featuring the Marx Bothers, when battling crippling arthritis and credited this habit to reducing the inflammation and pain in his body. Cousins wrote a book about the experience—*Anatomy of an Illness*—and ended up living years beyond what his doctors predicted.

I believe Jungian and shamanic techniques for healing, as well as other expanded-awareness practices, turn on the parasympathetic nervous system, lowering brain wave frequency and cortisol levels, along with reducing inflammation. Switching off the sympathetic nervous system, switching on the parasympathetic nervous system, and achieving integrated brain processing could turn out to be why energy medicine seems to be effective.

Another possible mechanism by which energy medicine might work is by keeping telomeres (structures at the ends of chromosomes) long, as we know chronic stress shortens telomeres and ages the body. These structures determine how often cells can reproduce, thereby keeping the body alive.

The greater the stress, the faster the telomeres shorten, like a candle wick burning until at last, there is no more wick to burn.

We do not know how to safely stop or repair telomeres via medications, unfortunately. However, we do have evidence that exercise, stress reduction or management, social support, and nutritional interventions and dietary changes show promise for reversing the deleterious effect of stress on our telomeres. These alterations may even lengthen them, extending our healthy lifespan.[8]

The Energy-Mind-Body Connection

There are other possible explanations for the observable effects of emotional and mental stress on physical wellness—and energy medicine's apparent effectiveness in treating the physical body. Cell biologist James L. Oschman, PhD, author of *Energy Medicine: The Scientific Basis,* points out that our bodies' cells and tissues vibrate and have electromagnetic properties. He suggests that the human body can be thought of as a "symphony of vibration"[9] and that vibrational energy from outside the body, such as that coming to it as a result of energy medicine interventions, might "affect the body's systems by working with and restoring balance to vibratory circuits."[10]

He also writes, "[L]iving matter is highly organized and exceedingly sensitive to the information conveyed by coherent signals. Coherent signals recognize no boundaries ... they are likely to serve as signals that integrate processes, such as growth, injury repair, defense, and the functioning of the organism as a whole." Perhaps these energetic changes directly affect cells and the hormonal stress response. He notes that cells communicate primarily through electromagnetic signals that underlie chemical interactions, and it's these "whispers" between cells that help them maintain their organization and function.[11]

Oschman's ideas about vibrational energy fit with those of shamans, who believe that we can access and work with healing energies when we alter our state of mind and allow our consciousness to "journey" or travel to places such as the lower world and upper world to gain energies and insights helpful for healing.

As I explained in the introduction to this book, these transpersonal realms are accessible to all of us if we shift our consciousness and enter a trancelike state. In this state, we are probably experiencing integrated brain processing, an experience that understandably creates a sense of oneness, unity, or harmony, since it involves coherent brain wave patterns and improved communication between many parts of the brain.

A Jungian might explain travel to transpersonal realms while in a trance-like state as the experiences conjured up by the mind because we have opened the door to the unconscious, where one can interact with inner figures and symbols as well as other representations of archetypal energies. Could it be that in a state of integrated brain processing, we access our ability to tap into the collective unconscious or transpersonal realms where past, present, and future run together?

Jungian psychology acknowledges its overlap with shamanism[12] and the importance of being in "right relationship" with the various parts of ourselves as well as with the unmanifest, unseen worlds that both traditions acknowledge, such as the collective unconscious. ("Right relationship" is a Buddhist concept that I think fits with the Jungian perspective.) Shamans strive toward *ayni*, which means "harmonious, reciprocal relationships"— with themselves and the various aspects of themselves, as well as with others, the natural world, and the invisible world.

Both traditions recognize a coherence between what we are experiencing within our brains and bodies and something happening outside of our individual consciousness. Carl Jung wrote: "A wrong functioning of the psyche can do much to injure the body, just as, conversely, a bodily illness can affect the psyche; for psyche and body are not separate entities but one and the same life. Thus, there is seldom a bodily ailment that does not show psychic complications, even if it is not psychically caused."[13]

In her book *Celtic Queen Maeve and Addiction,* Jungian Sylvia Perera suggests that disease and addiction may result from not experiencing a joyous sense of connection to the divine.[14] Shamans would agree that there is a spiritual component to illness, and that healing requires a reconnection to the numinous realms. Using expanded-awareness practices can help you feel a powerful sense of interconnectedness with Spirit, Source, or God—whatever name you use to describe this consciousness.

Whether or not you believe in God, you may find that using the expanded-awareness practices in this book, and other similar techniques for accessing your unconscious, will lead you to experience your individual consciousness as part of a larger consciousness that is always present.

I believe this larger, universal consciousness is the source of wisdom and archetypal energies that we can access and use to improve our lives.

I also believe that if you recognize your interconnectedness with Source, you may find it much easier to break out of denial and powerlessness, and instead be empowered to write a new and better story for your health.

Overlaps among shamanism, Jungianism, and neuroscience suggest some interesting questions about using trancelike states, as part of expanded-awareness practices, for healing work. What if our beliefs, which are integral to our stories, could be changed by interacting with a massive energy matrix to bring in new, archetypal energies shared by billions of human beings over the course of human history? Could the energies we access actually change our beliefs and our perceptions? What if we could experience these archetypal energies differently, or less intensely, because of our work in transpersonal realms? What if we were able to bring in the energy of perseverance, perhaps represented as a mouse and perceived as a spirit animal? This energy might free us from feeling overwhelmed and help us make small yet significant changes in our habits, such as taking a daily walk, that lead to progress over time.

As this book has shown, it is possible to dialogue with what we find in our unconscious and thus glean further insights into our health and alter our relationships with archetypal energies. We can dialogue with our diseases and their symptoms as well with as our inner healers. All of this can lead to transformation of our personal energy fields, allowing us to write and live according to a new story of our health.

End Notes

INTRODUCTION

1. The body's innate healing ability. Andrew Weil, MD, *Spontaneous Healing: How to Discover and Embrace Your Body's Natural Ability to Heal and Maintain Itself* (New York: Fawcett Columbine, 1995), 5.

CHAPTER 1

1. Summary of Ellen Langer research study. *Newsweek* staff, "Can We Reverse Aging by Changing How We Think?" *Newsweek* April 13, 2009, *http://www.newsweek.com/can-we-reverse-aging-changing-how-we-think-77669.*
2. The archetype of the warrior, who fights for something larger than himself, appears in *King, Warrior, Magician, Lover: Rediscovering the Archetypes of the Mature Masculine* (New York: HarperOne, 1991) by Robert Moore and Douglas Gillette.
3. Hospitals are devising stress-screening tools. Kay Manning, "Treating the Patient, Not Just the Cancer," *Chicago Tribune,* April 30, 2014.

CHAPTER 2

1. Seven chakras from the Hindu tradition. See: C.W. Leadbeater, *The Chakras* (Adyan, India: Theosophical Publishing House, 1927). Leadbeater does not offer associations that other writers on chakras have identified. For example, personal power is associated with the third chakra in Anodea Judith, *Wheels of Life: A User's Guide to the Chakra System* (Woodbury, MN: Llewellyn Publications, 1987).
2. Denise Gimenez Ramos, *The Psyche of the Body: A Jungian Approach to Psychosomatics* (Essex, England: Brunner-Routledge, 2004), 129.
3. Ibid., 85. Beth's story is detailed on pages 76–85.

CHAPTER 3

1. Eat food. Not too much. Mostly plants. Michael Pollan, *In Defense of Food: An Eater's Manifesto* (New York: Penguin Books, 2009), 1.

2. Sitting increases health risks for more than a dozen conditions. Sumathi Reddy, "The Price We Pay for Sitting Too Much," *Wall Street Journal*, September 28, 2015, *http://www.wsj.com/articles/the-price-we-pay-for-sitting-too-much-1443462015*.

3. Lack of exercise and too much sitting take a toll on physical health. Neville Owen et al., "Sedentary Behavior: Emerging Evidence for a New Health Risk." *Mayo Clinic Proceedings* 85.12 (2010): 1138–1141. PMC. Web. 27 July 2016. *http://www.ncbi.nlm.nih.gov/pmc/articles/PMC2996155/*.

4. Ways to reduce health risks of sitting all day. Patti Neighmond, "Sitting All Day: Worse for You Than You Might Think," *NPR Morning Edition*. April 25, 2011, *http://www.npr.org/2011/04/25/135575490/sitting-all-day-worse-for-you-than-you-might-think*. See also Bonnie Berkowitz and Patterson Clark, "The Health Hazards of Sitting," *Washington Post*, January 20, 2014, *https://www.washingtonpost.com/apps/g/page/national/the-health-hazards-of-sitting/750/* and Joseph Mercola, "Sitting Kills, Moving Heals" *mercola.com*, June 23, 2013, *http://articles.mercola.com/sites/articles/archive/2013/06/23/vernikos-sitting-kills.aspx*.

5. Jeanie Lerche Davis, "Anorexia Is Hitting Older Women," *webmd.com*, July 13, 2004, *http://www.webmd.com/mental-health/eating-disorders/anorexia-nervosa/features/anorexia-is-hitting-older-women*.

6. Assessing the body's true needs. Marion Woodman, *Addiction to Perfection: The Still Unravished Bride: A Psychological Study* (Toronto, Canada: Inner City Books, 1988), 56. "The ego must learn to ask the questions which the body is ready to answer in an unmistakably clear voice: 'What are my real needs? I betrayed myself in that meeting today. What did I really want to do? What does my body want to eat? Does it want to exercise? What would feed my spirit instead of my flesh? How can I make this heap of flesh my body? Do I love my body? Do I want to live? Do I want to enter life?'"

CHAPTER 4

1. Altered states are often associated with well-being. Arne Dietrich, "Functional Neuroanatomy of Altered States of Consciousness: The Transient Hypofrontality Hypothesis," *Consciousness and Cognition* 12 (2003): 231-56.

2. David Perlmutter, MD, and Alberto Villoldo, PhD, *Power Up Your Brain: The Neuroscience of Enlightenment* (Carlsbad, CA: Hay House, 2012), 153.

3.   Using an empty chair in the process of dialoguing is similar to a technique from Gestalt therapy. For more about the empty chair technique in Gestalt therapy, see, for example, *Counselling and Therapy Techniques: Theory and Practice,* Chapter 4, (Thousand Oaks, CA: SAGE Publishing, 2011) by Augustine Meier and Micheline Biovin; also Carl Greer, PhD, PsyD, *Change Your Story, Change Your Life: Using Shamanic and Jungian Tools to Achieve Personal Transformation* (Scotland: Findhorn Press, 2014), 108.

4.   Marion Woodman, *Addiction to Perfection: The Still Unravished Bride* (Toronto, Ontario, Canada: Inner City Books, 1982), 79.

5.   For more on dreams and their health predictive qualities, see Michelle Carr, "Do Your Dreams Predict Your Health," *Psychology Today,* December 12, 2014, *https://www.psychologytoday.com/blog/dream-factory/201412/do-your-dreams-predict-your-health.*

6.   Andrea Brown, "Taking Small Steps Pays Off, Northwestern Health Study Says," *Chicago Tribune,* July 11, 2012, *http://www.chicagotribune.com/lifestyles/health/ct-x-couch-potato-study-20120711-story.html.*

CHAPTER 5

1.   Anne Tergesen, "To Age Well, Change How You Feel About Aging," *Wall Street Journal,* October 19, 2015, *http://www.wsj.com/articles/to-age-well-change-how-you-feel-about-aging-1445220002.*

2.   Mark Hyman, MD, *The UltraMind Solution: Fix Your Broken Brain by Healing Your Body First* (New York: Scribner, 2010), 38.

3.   Cancer sometimes reverses itself. See: Gina Kolata, "Cancers Can Vanish Without Treatment, But How?" *New York Times,* October 26, 2009, *http://www.nytimes.com/2009/10/27/health/27canc.html.*

4.   It isn't just women concerned about the role of cancer screening tests. See: Gina Kolata, "More Men With Early Prostate Cancer Are Choosing to Avoid Treatment," *New York Times,* May 24, 2016, *http://www.nytimes.com/2016/05/25/health/prostate-cancer-active-surveillance-surgery-radiation.html.*

5.   Kristin Della Volpe, "News Update: Can Kale Cause Thyroid Cancer?" *Endocrineweb.com,* updated March 16, 2016, *http://www.endocrineweb.com/conditions/hypothyroidism/news-update-can-kale-cause-hypothyroidism.*

CHAPTER 6

1.   Edward Tick, "Shamanism and War-Induced Post-Traumatic Stress Disorder," in *Spirited Medicine: Shamanism in Contemporary Healthcare,* ed. Cecile Carson (Baltimore, MD: Otter Bay Books, 2013), 249.

2. Nature reduces depression. Carol Sorgen, "Do You Need a Nature Prescription?" webmd.com, June 19, 2013, *http://www.webmd.com/balance/features/nature-therapy-ecotherapy.*

3. Shinrin-yoku is Japanese for "forest bathing." See: *http://www.shinrin-yoku.org/.* See also Emi Morita, Makoto Imai, Masako Okawa, Tomiyasu Miyaura and Soichiro Miyazaki, "A Before and After Comparison of the Effects of Forest Walking on the Sleep of a Community-based Sample of People with Sleep Complaints," *BioPsychoSocial Medicine: The Official Journal of the Japanese Society of Psychosomatic Medicine,* 5, no. 13 (2011). doi:10.1186/1751-0759-5-13. And also, International Society of Nature and Forest Medicine, list of recommended articles and books, *http://www.infom.org/paperandbooks/index.html.*

4. Eva M. Selhub, MD, and Alan C. Logan, ND, *Your Brain on Nature: The Science of Nature's Influence on Your Health, Happiness, and Vitality* (Toronto, Ontario: Collins, 2014), 12. See also Eva Selhub and Alan Logan, "Your Brain on Nature: Forest Bathing and Reduced Stress," January 8, 2013, *http://www.motherearthnews.com/natural-health/herbal-remedies/forest-bathing-ze0z1301zgar.aspx?PageId=3.*

5. Negative ions reduce depression. Denise Mann, "Negative Ions Create Positive Vibes," *webmd.com,* May 6, 2002, *http://www.webmd.com/balance/features/negative-ions-create-positive-vibes.*

6. David Perlmutter, MD, *Brain Maker: The Power of Gut Microbes to Heal and Protect Your Brain for Life.* (Boston: Little, Brown and Company, 2015), 201. This book, along with *Power Up Your Brain: The Neuroscience of Enlightenment* (Carlsbad, CA: Hay House, 2012) written by David Perlmutter, MD, and Alberto Villoldo, PhD, offers information about the relationship between microbes in the gut and our brain's health and functioning. Also, note that according to Alberto Villoldo, PhD, "Our bodies contain over 600 varieties of microbes from nature." From Alberto Villoldo, PhD, *One Spirit Medicine: Ancient Ways to Ultimate Wellness* (Carlsbad, CA: Hay House, 2015) 37–38.

7. Gardening has health benefits. G. Davies, M. Devereaux, M. Lennartsson, U. Schmutz, & S. Williams, *The Benefits of Gardening and Food Growing for Health and Wellbeing* by Garden Organic and Sustain, Coventry and London, UK, American Horticultural Association (April 2014), *http://www.farmtocafeteriacanada.ca/wp-content/uploads/2014/06/GrowingHealth_BenefitsReport.pdf.*

8.   Fluorescent lighting may cause increase in eye diseases. Helen L. Walls, Kelvin L. Walls, and Geza Benke, "Eye Disease Resulting From Increased Use of Fluorescent Lighting as a Climate Change Mitigation Strategy." *American Journal of Public Health* 101, no. 12 (2011): 2222–25, *http://www.ncbi.nlm.nih.gov/pmc/articles/PMC3222423/*.

9.   Christopher D. Zevitas and Jonathan D. Cybulski (Volpe National Transportation Systems Center) and Eileen McNeely (Harvard School of Public Health) "Evaluating the Health Benefits of Natural Sounds: An Approach for Assessing the Environmental Impacts of Transportation Noise," *http://ntl.bts.gov/lib/45000/45800/45892/Zevitas_Natural-Sounds.pdf*

10. Henry David Thoreau, *Walden; or, Life in the Woods* (Mineola, New York: Dover Publications, 1995), 121.

11. C.G. Jung, Meredith Sabini, ed., and Joseph Henderson, MD, *The Earth Has a Soul: C. G. Jung on Nature, Technology and Modern Life* (Berkeley, CA: North Atlantic Books, 2002), 58.

12. J. J. Alvarsson, S. Wiens, and M. E. Nilsson, "Stress Recovery During Exposure to Nature Sound and Environmental Noise." *International Journal of Environmental Research and Public Health* 7, no. 3 (2010): 1036–46, *http://doi.org/10.3390/ijerph7031036*.

13. Health benefits of living in urban areas near nature. American Institute of Biological Sciences, "Could a Dose of Nature Be Just What the Doctor Ordered?" *ScienceDaily, www.sciencedaily.com/releases/2015/04/150408124616.htm*.

14. Surgery patients may recover more quickly. Roger Ulrich, "View through a Window May Influence Recovery," *Science,* 224.4647 (April 27, 1984), 224–25.

15. Adam Alter, "How Nature Resets Our Minds and Bodies," *The Atlantic,* March 29, 2013, *http://www.theatlantic.com/health/archive/2013/03/how-nature-resets-our-minds-and-bodies/274455/*.

16. Jung quote on observing how the picture unfolds, taken from a 1947 letter of his, found in *Encountering Jung on Active Imagination,* ed. Joan Chodorow (Routledge, NJ: Princeton University Press, 1997), 164.

17. Tove Fjeld, "The Effect of Interior Planting on Health and Discomfort Among Workers and School Children," *HortTechnology* 10, no. 1 (January-March 2000): 46–52, *http://horttech.ashspublications.org/content/10/1/46.full.pdf+html*.

18. Gretchen Reynolds, "How Walking in Nature Changes the Brain," *New York Times*, July 22, 2015, *http://well.blogs.nytimes.com/2015/07/22/how-nature-changes-the-brain/?action=click&contentCollection=U.S.&module=MostEmailed&version=Full&region=Marginalia&src=me&pgtype=article*.

19. Brain waves, the parasympathetic nervous system, and integration between the prefrontal cortex and your emotional center are explored in Michael Winkelman, *Shamanism: A Biopsychosocial Paradigm* (Santa Barbara, CA: ABC-CLIO/Praeger, 2009), 181.

CHAPTER 7

1. Carl Jung, "Archetypes of the Collective Unconscious," in *Collected Works of C. G. Jung, Vol. 9, Part 1: Archetypes and the Collective Unconscious,* edited and translated by Gerhard Adler and F. C. Hull (Princeton, NJ: Princeton University Press, 1959 and 1969), 18–19. "Water is the commonest symbol for the unconscious… Water is earthy and tangible; it is also the fluid of the instinct-driven body, blood, and the flowing of blood, the odour of the beast, carnality heavy with passion."

CHAPTER 8

1. "Stress by Generation." APA Press release. *Stress in America 2012. http://www.apa.org/news/press/releases/stress/2012/generations.aspx.*

2. Anne Tergesen, "To Age Well, Change How You Feel About Aging," *Wall Street Journal,* October 19, 2015, *http://www.wsj.com/articles/to-age-well-change-how-you-feel-about-aging-1445220002.*

3. Diane E. Meier, "Increased Access to Palliative Care and Hospice Services: Opportunities to Improve Value in Health Care," *The Milbank Quarterly* 89, no. 3 (2011): 343–80, *http://doi.org/10.1111/j.1468-0009.2011.00632.x.*

4. Anne Tergesen, "To Age Well, Change How You Feel About Aging," *Wall Street Journal,* October 19, 2015, *http://www.wsj.com/articles/to-age-well-change-how-you-feel-about-aging-1445220002.*

AFTERWORD

1. Aaron E. Carroll, "Labels Like Alternative Medicine Don't Matter. The Science Does." *New York Times,* August 10, 2015. See also Anahad O'Connor, "Acupuncture Provides True Pain Relief in Study," *New York Times*, September 11, 2012.

2. Lissa Rankin's Facebook page, August 5, 2013, accessed July 1, 2016, *https://www.facebook.com/lissarankin/posts/666094616753296.*

3. Impoverished information. Denise Gimenez Ramos, *The Psyche of the Body: A Jungian Approach to Psychosomatics* (Essex, England: Brunner-Routledge, 2004), 131-132.

4. Michael Winkelman, *Shamanism: A Biopsychosocial Paradigm*, 2nd ed. (Santa Barbara, CA: ABC-CLIO/Praeger, 2009) 25, citing J. M., Davidson, "The Physiology of Meditation and Mystical States of Consciousness," *Perspectives in Biology and Medicine* 19, no. 3 (Spring 1976): 345–79.

5. Federation of American Societies for Experimental Biology (FASEB). "Fight Memory Loss with a Smile (or Chuckle)," *ScienceDaily.* April 27, 2014, *www.sciencedaily.com/releases/2014/04/140427185149.htm.*

6. Mayo Clinic Staff, "Stress Relief from Laughter? It's No Joke," *mayoclinic.org,* April 21, 2016, *http://www.mayoclinic.org/healthy-lifestyle/stress-management/in-depth/stress-relief/art-20044456.*

7. American Physiological Society. "Anticipating a Laugh Reduces Our Stress Hormones, Study Shows." *ScienceDaily.* April 4, 2008. *www.sciencedaily.com/releases/2008/04/080407114617.htm.*

8. Elizabeth Fernandez, "Lifestyle Changes May Lengthen Telomeres, A Measure of Cell Aging," UCSF News Center, *ucsf.edu.* September 16, 2013, *https://www.ucsf.edu/news/2013/09/108886/lifestyle-changes-may-lengthen-telomeres-measure-cell-aging.*

9. James L. Oschman, *Energy Medicine: The Scientific Basis* (London: Churchill Livingstone, 2000), 123.

10. Ibid., 62.

11. Ibid., 251.

12. John Merchant, *Shamans and Analysts: New Insights on the Wounded Healer* (East Sussex, England: Routledge, 2012). On p. 1, Merchant writes, "At the Fourteenth International Congress for Analytical Psychology's symposium on training, for which the theme was 'What makes a good analyst?', [Adolf] Guggenbuhl-Craig (1999) alluded to a 'shaman archetype' as one which is likely to be present in an analyst regarded as 'good.' In so doing he placed shamanism as conceptually central to analytic work." And on p. 3, he cites another Jungian analyst, C. J. Groesbeck, saying, "Groesbeck (1989, p. 274) goes so far as to say that it is only those who 'function as shamans in the therapeutic process dealing directly with the patient's illness in order to produce a transformational healing experience' who can be considered the 'true Jungians'." See C. J. Groesbeck, "C. G. Jung and the Shaman's Vision," *Journal of Analytical Psychology* 1989, 34: 255-275. doi:10.1111/j.1465-5922.1989.00255.x.

13. Jung, C. G., *Collected Works of C. G. Jung: The First Complete English Edition.* Ed. Sir Herbert Read. (Princeton, NJ: Routledge Press, 2014), 2759.

14. Sylvia Perera, *Celtic Queen Maeve and Addiction: An Archetypal Perspective* (Lake Worth, Florida: Nicolas-Hays, 2001), 18, 167–169. "[Maeve] represents the profound and archetypal need for experiences of ecstasy and the transformative fullness of emotion and vision such experiences may produce." (p. 18) and "[When] we cannot relate consciously and reverently to the energies we image as Maeve, we may find ourselves drawn unconsciously into her field and caught in 'blind bondage to archetypal factors.' ... Jung has stressed that we can become aware of every archetypal energy field via its imaginal and energic aspects (including somatic and emotional ones)... With more conscious access to the archetypal energic processes, we may discover how to relate to the patterns within them as they structure matter and mind, body, and spirit. Thus we can begin to learn to work with and within the physical, emotional, mental, and spiritual potencies as these manifest in our lives. The symbolic image reveals the structure of the underlying archetypal energy pattern that creates health and potential meaning when it is relatively balanced. Equally it provides clues to rebalance the skewed complexes built around the archetypal core that embody the disease. Through the symbol we can thus gain access to the archetypal patterns that support health... " (pp. 167–168).

Bibliography

Bailey, Alice. *A Treatise on White Magic, or The Way of the Disciple*. New York: Lucis Publishing Company, 1934.

Carson, Cecile. ed. *Spirited Medicine: Shamanism in Contemporary Healthcare*. Baltimore, MD: Otter Bay Books, 2013.

Gimenez Ramos, Denise. *The Psyche of the Body: A Jungian Approach to Psychosomatics*. Essex, England: Brunner-Routledge, 2004.

Greer, Carl, PhD, PsyD. *Change Your Story, Change Your Life: Using Shamanic and Jungian Tools to Achieve Personal Transformation*. Scotland: Findhorn Press, 2014.

Hyman, Mark, MD. *The UltraMind Solution: Fix Your Broken Brain by Healing Your Body First*. New York: Scribner, 2010.

Judith, Anodea. *Wheels of Life: A User's Guide to the Chakra System*. Woodbury, MN: Llewellyn Publications, 1987.

Jung, C. G. *Collected Works of C. G. Jung: The First Complete English Edition*. Edited by Sir Herbert Read. Princeton, NJ: Routledge Press, 2014.

——— *Jung on Active Imagination*. Edited by Joan Chodorow. Routledge, NJ: Princeton University Press, 1997, 164.

——— "Archetypes of the Collective Unconscious," in *Collected Works of C. G. Jung, Vol. 9, Part 1: Archetypes and the Collective Unconscious*. Edited and translated by Gerhard Adler and F. C. Hull. Princeton, New Jersey: Princeton University Press, 1959 and 1969.

——— *The Earth Has a Soul: C. G. Jung on Nature, Technology and Modern Life*. Edited by Meredith Sabini and Joseph Henderson, MD, Berkeley, CA: North Atlantic Books, 2002, 58.

Leadbeater, C.W. *The Chakras*. Adyan, India: Theosophical Publishing House, 1927.

Meier, Augustine, and Micheline Boivin. *Counseling and Therapy Techniques: Theory and Practice*. Thousand Oaks, CA: SAGE Publishing, 2011.

Merchant, John. *Shamans and Analysts: New Insights on the Wounded Healer*. East Sussex, England: Routledge, 2012.

Moore, Robert, and Douglas Gillette. *King, Warrior, Magician, Lover: Rediscovering the Archetypes of the Mature Masculine.* New York: HarperOne, 1991.

Nichols, Wallace J. *Blue Mind: The Surprising Science That Shows How Being Near, In, On, or Under Water Can Make You Happier, Healthier, More Connected, and Better At What You Do.* New York: Little, Brown and Company, 2014.

Oschman, James L., PhD, *Energy Medicine: The Scientific Basis.* London: Churchill Livingstone, 2000.

Perlmutter, David, MD. *Brain Maker: The Power of Gut Microbes to Heal and Protect Your Brain for Life.* Boston: Little, Brown and Company, 2015.

Perlmutter, David, MD, and Alberto Villoldo, PhD. *Power Up Your Brain: The Neuroscience of Enlightenment.* Carlsbad, CA: Hay House, 2012.

Perera, Sylvia. *Celtic Queen Maeve and Addiction: An Archetypal Perspective.* York Beach, ME: Nicolas-Hays, Inc., 2001.

Ramos, Denise Gimenez. *The Psyche of the Body: A Jungian Approach to Psychosomatics.* Essex, England: Brenner-Routledge, 2004.

Rankin, Lissa. *Mind Over Medicine: Scientific Proof That You Can Heal Yourself.* Carlsbad, CA: Hay House, 2013.

Pollan, Michael. *In Defense of Food: An Eater's Dilemma.* New York: Penguin Books, 2009.

Selhub, Eva M., MD, and Alan C. Logan, ND. *Your Brain on Nature: The Science of Nature's Influence on Your Health, Happiness, and Vitality.* Toronto, Ontario: Collins, 2014.

Thoreau, Henry David. *Walden; or, Life in the Woods.* Mineola, New York: Dover Publications, 1995.

Villoldo, Alberto, PhD. *One Spirit Medicine: Ancient Ways to Ultimate Wellness.* Carlsbad, CA: Hay House, 2015.

—— *Shaman, Healer Sage: How to Heal Yourself and Others with the Energy Medicine of the Americas.* New York: Harmony Books, 2000.

Weil, Andrew, MD. *Spontaneous Healing: How to Discover and Embrace Your Body's Natural Ability to Heal and Maintain Itself.* New York: Fawcett Columbine, 1995.

Winkelman, Michael. *Shamanism: A Biopsychosocial Paradigm.* Santa Barbara, CA: ABC-CLIO/Praeger, 2009.

Woodman, Marion. *Addiction to Perfection: The Still Unravished Bride: A Psychological Study.* Toronto, Canada: Inner City Books, 1988.

Also of interest from Findhorn Press

CHANGE YOUR STORY, CHANGE YOUR LIFE

CARL GREER

CHANGE YOUR STORY, CHANGE YOUR LIFE is a practical self-help guide to personal transformation using traditional shamanic techniques combined with journaling and Carl Greer's method for dialoguing that draws upon Jungian active imagination. The exercises inspire readers to work with insights and energies derived during the use of modalities that tap into the unconscious so that they may consciously choose the changes they would like to make in their lives and begin implementing them.

978-1-84409-464-6

FINDHORN PRESS

Life-Changing Books

For a complete catalogue,
please contact:

Findhorn Press Ltd
117-121 High Street,
Forres IV36 1AB,
Scotland, UK

t +44 (0)1309 690582
f +44 (0)131 777 2711
e info@findhornpress.com

or consult our catalogue online
(with secure order facility) at
www.findhornpress.com

For information on the Findhorn Foundation:
www.findhorn.org